Daethon & Arundel

A Ballet in Four Acts

David Hotchkiss

Published by Clink Street Publishing 2018

First edition.

ISBNs:
978-1-912562-09-1 paperback
978-1-912562-10-7 ebook

For Carlotta, Sophie, Maddie, Ailsa, Josh, Verity and most of all Karen

Who taught me so much, and saved me, without even knowing it

The Players

Daethon – A Servant

Prince Arundel

The Dark Lord Ambrogio – Lord of the Vampires and Great Grandson of Vlad Tepes

Gullveig the Harpy – A Witch

Princess Lorelle

Prince Udolf de Marenne

The Lady Nerida

King Haelan

Macon the Blacksmith

The Nobles x 8

The Ladies-in-Waiting x 8

The Vampires x 6

The Spirits x 6

The Servants x 5

OVERTURE

The Overture plays as the lights go down and then in the pitch blackness, projected against the curtain, comes the title and images of all the lead characters one by one, short momentary clips of each of them looking proudly into the distance up to Bar 18. The lights then go dark and a deep red fills the stage, the red of blood. At Bar 65 the red fades away to nothing before the curtain is then backlit in bright white light. A ballet in silhouette now proceeds, telling through silhouette only a precis of the tale to come. The ballet in silhouette is to be filled with form and beauty to convey the music and prepare the audience for what is to come. As the ballet in silhouette ends in Bar 85 the backlighting goes down and for the remainder of the Overture the curtain is lit from the front with dark red and the flashes and sounds of a dark storm brewing.

The stage is then set and the ballet can begin…

♩= 120
Flute
Oboe
Clarinet in B♭
Bassoon
Horn in F
p
mp
Trumpet in B♭
p
mp
Tuba
p
f
Timpani
p
f
Cymbals
Choir
♩= 120
Violin I
f
Violin II
p
mp
Viola
p
mp
Violoncello
p
f
Double Bass
p
f

6
Fl.
Ob.
Cl.
mp
Bsn.
mp
Hn.
Tpt.
Tba.
Timp.
Cym.
Choir
Vln. I
Vln. II
Vla.
Vc.
Db.

10
Fl.
mf
Ob.
mf
Cl.
mf
Bsn.
mf
Hn.
Tpt.
Tba.
Timp.
Cym.
Choir
Vln. I
Vln. II
f
Vla.
Vc.
Db.

14
Fl.
Ob.
Cl.
Bsn.
Hn.
Tpt.
Tba.
Timp.
Cym.
Choir
Vln. I
Vln. II
Vla.
Vc.
Db.

18

Fl.
f

Ob.
f

Cl.
f

Bsn.
f

Hn.
mf

Tpt.
mf

Tba.
mf

Timp.
tr

Cym.
f

Choir
mf
mf

Vln. I
mf

Vln. II
mf

Vla.
f

Vc.
f

Db.
f

26
molto rall.
Fl.
Ob.
Cl.
Bsn.
Hn.
Tpt.
Tba.
Timp.
Cym.
Choir
molto rall.
Vln. I
Vln. II
Vla.
Vc.
Db.

35
♩= 65
Fl.
mp
Ob.
Cl.
Bsn.
Hn.
Tpt.
Tba.
Timp.
Cym.
Choir
♩= 65
Vln. I
Vln. II
Vla.
Vc.
Db.

41
Fl.
Ob.
mp
Cl.
mp
Bsn.
Hn.
Tpt.
Tba.
Timp.
Cym.
Choir
Vln. I
mp
Vln. II
Vla.
Vc.
Db.

47
Fl.
Ob.
Cl.
Bsn.
Hn.
Tpt.
Tba.
Timp.
Cym.
Choir
Vln. I
Vln. II
Vla.
Vc.
Db.

52
Fl.
Ob.
Cl.
Bsn.
Hn.
Tpt.
Tba.
Timp.
Cym.
Choir
Vln. I
Vln. II
Vla.
Vc.
Db.
p
mp

60

Fl.
Ob.
Cl.
Bsn.
Hn.
Tpt.
Tba.
Timp.
Cym.
Choir
Vln. I
Vln. II
Vla.
Vc.
Db.

mp mp mp mp mp p mp mf mp mf mp mf

65
Fl.
Ob.
Cl.
Bsn.
Hn.
Tpt.
Tba.
Timp.
tr
f
Cym.
f
Choir
Vln. I
Vln. II
Vla.
Vc.
Db.

70

Fl.

Ob.

Cl.

Bsn.

Hn.

Tpt.

Tba.

Timp.

Cym.

Choir

Vln. I

Vln. II

Vla.

Vc.

Db.

75
Fl.
Ob.
Cl.
Bsn.
Hn.
Tpt.
Tba.
Timp.
Cym.
Choir
Vln. I
Vln. II
Vla.
Vc.
Db.
mf
mp

80
molto rall.
Fl.
Ob.
Cl.
Bsn.
Hn.
Tpt.
Tba.
Timp.
Cym.
Choir
molto rall.
Vln. I
Vln. II
Vla.
Vc.
Db.
p
tr

86
♩ = 100
Fl.
Ob.
Cl.
Bsn.
Hn.
Tpt.
Tba.
Timp.
(tr)
Cym.
Choir
♩ = 100
Vln. I
Vln. II
Vla.
Vc.
Db.
mf

94
Fl.
Ob.
Cl.
Bsn.
Hn.
Tpt.
Tba.
Timp.
Cym.
Choir
Vln. I
Vln. II
Vla.
Vc.
Db.

102

Fl. *mp*

Ob. *mp*

Cl. *mp*

Bsn. *mp*

Hn.

Tpt. *mp*

Tba. *mp*

Timp. *mp*

Cym.

Choir

Vln. I *mp*

Vln. II *mp*

Vla. *mp*

Vc. *mp*

Db. *mp*

111
Fl.
Ob.
Cl.
Bsn.
Hn.
Tpt.
Tba.
Timp.
Cym.
Choir
Vln. I
Vln. II
Vla.
Vc.
Db.
mf

120
Fl.
Ob.
Cl.
Bsn.
Hn.
Tpt.
Tba.
Timp.
Cym.
Choir
Vln. I
Vln. II
Vla.
Vc.
Db.

128
Fl.
Ob.
Cl.
Bsn.
Hn.
Tpt.
Tba.
Timp.
Cym.
Choir
Vln. I
Vln. II
Vla.
Vc.
Db.
p

136
Fl.
Ob.
Cl.
Bsn.
Hn.
Tpt.
Tba.
Timp.
Cym.
Choir
Vln. I
Vln. II
Vla.
Vc.
Db.

144
rall.
Fl.
ff
Ob.
ff
Cl.
ff
Bsn.
ff
Hn.
mp
Tpt.
mp
Tba.
ff
tr
Timp.
ff
Cym.
Choir
rall.
Vln. I
ff
Vln. II
ff
Vla.
ff
Vc.
ff
Db.
ff

151
Fl.
Ob.
Cl.
Bsn.
Hn.
Tpt.
Tba.
Timp.
Cym.
Choir
Vln. I
Vln. II
Vla.
Vc.
Db.
pp
pp

ACT I

ACT I

Scene I – A Week Before the Feast

Daethon toils with his fellow servants who are preparing for the return of King Haelan and his family. His daily life is filled with the drudgery of servitude, but he is a dreamer, and as he works he is constantly distracted into dreams. As the dark overture finishes and the scene opens Daethon is polishing boots in the corner whilst the other servants clean and dance with their brooms. The musical rhythm conveys the constant ticking of the clock as the time wears on, but as Daethon's mind wanders into dreams the surroundings fade away and he dances in his imagination in the spotlight of his mind; he dances to show just how much he desires the Prince and does all this by expressing his feelings for the boot he is holding, until suddenly his dream is broken when the Head of the Household comes in. The Head of the Household roughly disciplines Daethon for his clumsiness, and as the scene ends Daethon once more resumes his musings and with boot in hand as a representation of his love he is standing on stage, only to get a clip round the ear from the Head of the Household with the final note of the piece before he shuffles off stage with the Head of the Household shaking his head behind him.

Choreography, Costume and Set Notes

- The setting is 18th Century, with all the flourish and gaiety of the Austrian Court; the kingdom is an obscure alpine province and King Haelan rules over lands lying between the kingdoms of the Austrian princes and the Hungarian lords.

- As noted the scene starts in one of the bedrooms of the palace; a large wooden four-poster bed lies up centre stage with other pieces of furniture stage right and stage left, leaving a central space to dance.

- The Head of the Household is to be dressed austerely in black; Daethon's clothes as a servant can be white and sackcloth and simple; only later will his true colours emerge and for now they are submerged beneath his life as a servant.

- The tubular bells in the piece are the ticking clock and guide the dance of the other servants; Daethon is seated stage left on a wooden chair polishing the boots; as Bar 17 starts he rises and holding one boot in hand moves to centre stage; the other servants steadily dance to the slower refrain, followed by then making their way to stage left and stage right to start polishing, weaving or doing other seated tasks as the staccato horn refrain brings the introduction to a close. The lights change as the second section begins in Bar 25; a soft circular light from above fills centre stage where Daethon dances a solo to the waltz with his boot, whilst around the stage the lights are dimmed down almost to nothing so that the other servants are hardly visible. It is as if in his dreamings Daethon is alone, even though he is in a crowded room.

- As typical for interior design of the period, choose a dominant colour and have it everywhere; the set needs to exude wealth since we are in the palace of the king.

- A comic air can be brought out with the rough treatment by the Head of the Household and a clip round the ear with the final note of Bar 138 is intended to produce a slight laugh from the audience as it takes Daethon by surprise and he expresses his hurt feelings in his face as he shuffles off stage.

- The Head of the Household shakes his head to the audience as the scene closes and lights go down as he is last to leave the stage.

♩ = 80
Piccolo
Flute
Oboe
Clarinet in B♭
Bassoon
Horn in F
Mellophone in F
Trumpet in C
Trumpet in B♭
Tuba
♩ = 80
Timpani
Tubular Bells
Violin I
Violin II
Violoncello
Double Bass

6
Picc.
Fl.
Ob.
Cl.
Bsn.
Hn.
Mln.
C Tpt.
Tpt.
Tba.
Timp.
Tub. B.
Vln. I
Vln. II
Vc.
Db.

10
Picc.
Fl.
Ob.
Cl.
Bsn.
Hn.
Mln.
C Tpt.
Tpt.
Tba.
Timp.
Tub. B.
Vln. I
Vln. II
Vc.
Db.

14
Picc.
Fl.
Ob.
Cl.
Bsn.
Hn.
Mln.
C Tpt.
Tpt.
Tba.
Timp.
Tub. B.
Vln. I
Vln. II
Vc.
Db.

rall.
♩ = 150
19
Picc.
Fl.
Ob.
Cl.
Bsn.
Hn.
Mln.
C Tpt.
Tpt.
Tba.
rall.
♩ = 150
Timp.
Tub. B.
Vln. I
Vln. II
Vc.
Db.

26
Picc.
Fl.
Ob.
Cl.
Bsn.
Hn.
Mln.
C Tpt.
Tpt.
Tba.
Timp.
Tub. B.
Vln. I
Vln. II
Vc.
Db.

35
Picc.
Fl.
Ob.
Cl.
Bsn.
Hn.
Mln.
C Tpt.
Tpt.
Tba.
Timp.
Tub. B.
Vln. I
Vln. II
Vc.
Db.

44
Picc.
Fl.
Ob.
Cl.
Bsn.
Hn.
Mln.
C Tpt.
Tpt.
Tba.
Timp.
Tub. B.
Vln. I
Vln. II
Vc.
Db.

53
Picc.
Fl.
Ob.
Cl.
Bsn.
Hn.
Mln.
C Tpt.
Tpt.
Tba.
Timp.
Tub. B.
Vln. I
Vln. II
Vc.
Db.

62
Picc.
Fl.
Ob.
Cl.
Bsn.
Hn.
Mln.
C Tpt.
Tpt.
Tba.
Timp.
Tub. B.
Vln. I
Vln. II
Vc.
Db.

71
Picc.
Fl.
Ob.
Cl.
Bsn.
Hn.
Mln.
C Tpt.
Tpt.
Tba.
Timp.
Tub. B.
Vln. I
Vln. II
Vc.
Db.

80
Picc.
Fl.
Ob.
Cl.
Bsn.
Hn.
Mln.
C Tpt.
Tpt.
Tba.
Timp.
Tub. B.
Vln. I
Vln. II
Vc.
Db.

89
Picc.
Fl.
Ob.
Cl.
Bsn.
Hn.
Mln.
C Tpt.
Tpt.
Tba.
Timp.
Tub. B.
Vln. I
Vln. II
Vc.
Db.

98
Picc.
Fl.
Ob.
Cl.
Bsn.
Hn.
Mln.
C Tpt.
Tpt.
Tba.
Timp.
Tub. B.
Vln. I
Vln. II
Vc.
Db.

107
Picc.
Fl.
Ob.
Cl.
Bsn.
Hn.
Mln.
C Tpt.
Tpt.
Tba.
Timp.
Tub. B.
Vln. I
Vln. II
Vc.
Db.

116
rall.
Picc.
Fl.
Ob.
Cl.
Bsn.
Hn.
Mln.
C Tpt.
Tpt.
Tba.
rall.
Timp.
Tub. B.
Vln. I
Vln. II
Vc.
Db.

125
♩ = 80

Picc.
Fl.
Ob.
Cl.
Bsn.
Hn.
Mln.
C Tpt.
Tpt.
Tba.

♩ = 80

Timp.
Tub. B.
Vln. I
Vln. II
Vc.
Db.

130
Picc.
Fl.
Ob.
Cl.
Bsn.
Hn.
Mln.
C Tpt.
Tpt.
Tba.
Timp.
Tub. B.
Vln. I
Vln. II
Vc.
Db.

134
Picc.
Fl.
Ob.
Cl.
Bsn.
Hn.
Mln.
C Tpt.
Tpt.
Tba.
Timp.
Tub. B.
Vln. I
Vln. II
Vc.
Db.

137
Picc.
Fl.
Ob.
Cl.
Bsn.
Hn.
Mln.
C Tpt.
Tpt.
Tba.
Timp.
Tub. B.
Vln. I
Vln. II
Vc.
Db.

ACT I

Scene II – The Great Hall

The Great Hall is set with the ready-makings for the great banquet, with a huge U-shaped table set with so many sumptuous things that one can hardly see for the food. The servants initially are dancing around making everything ready before the trumpets sound and they rush off to the corners of the hall to be ready in waiting. The nobles enter with their ladies, with much pomp, and once all are in the hall a great dance begins, to celebrate the start of the festivities; amongst the nobles and ladies are Prince Udolf de Marenne and the Lady Nerida. King Haelan enters with his son and daughter in tow, Prince Arundel and the Princess Lorelle. Daethon watches from behind one of the chairs, his vision captivated by the Prince. The nobles bow and acknowledge the King and his children, and Prince Udolf boldly gets down on one knee to kiss the hand of Princess Lorelle. Meanwhile the Prince is exploring the feast and his eyes across the table catch Daethon on his way around. He stops but then is pulled away into the centre of the hall by the Lady Nerida. The Lady Nerida attempts to beguile and enchant him with her beauty and her dance and Daethon sulks in the corner as she does so. The Prince dances with her but from time to time his gaze still wanders to Daethon, who in those brief moments captures the Prince's gaze before returning to his sulking. The Princess Lorelle and Prince Udolf skulk in a corner, whispering sweet nothings and laughing at the Prince and Nerida. Meanwhile, all the nobles join for dancing and Daethon tries to join in but gets overwhelmed and runs away; eventually all head off stage to leave Daethon alone in the empty hall. He mourns and expresses his love for Arundel in a short solo dance to the heavens. At the end he falls bereft into the middle of the hall in a spotlight with all the remaining lights around gone and the Great Hall faded away. In the darkness beyond the edge of the light there is a rustling and the new scene begins now away on a mountaintop in a dark cave.

Choreography, Costume and Set Notes

- The nobles are dressed in finery, King Haelan in gold with a mighty jewelled crown and chain, Arundel in brilliant sparkling white with a black cape, a sword and a fine subdued coronet, Daethon is in smarter clothes but still in peasant dress as a servant and Lorelle is dressed in yellow for this is her colour; throughout the ballet she is to always to be seen in different outfits but always in yellow; Udolf is in brown and Nerida in green. Haelan does not dance, he observes, greets and sits on the throne in the up centre stage; the place is to be lit with braziers and have a large U-shaped table arrangement about the throne, leaving the middle of the stage for dancing and acting.

- Daethon's eyes meet the Prince's in Bar 37 before the dance with Nerida, and Daethon is lost amongst the nobles getting increasingly muddled and overwhelmed in Bars 45 to 76 running away at the end of this, with the nobles all dancing off stage by Bar 92.

- Daethon's final mourning on his own to Bars 93 to 107 is to slightly dimmed light with a growing spotlight on him that ends with only the spotlight remaining on him in centre stage; a shadow curtain lowers and the spotlight goes dark blood red for the scene change, before raising onto Scene III where Daethon is still collapsed in place, but now in the cave of the vampires in the mountains.

♩ = 130
Piccolo
Flute
Oboe
Clarinet in B♭
Bassoon
Horn in F
Trumpet in C
Trombone
Tuba
Timpani
♩ = 130
Cymbals
Violin I
Violin II
Viola
Violoncello
Double Bass

6
Picc.
Fl.
Ob.
Cl.
Bsn.
Hn.
C Tpt.
Tbn.
Tba.
Timp.
Cym.
Vln. I
Vln. II
Vla.
Vc.
Db.

11
Picc.
Fl.
Ob.
Cl.
Bsn.
Hn.
C Tpt.
Tbn.
Tba.
Timp.
Cym.
Vln. I
Vln. II
Vla.
Vc.
Db.

16
Picc.
Fl.
Ob.
Cl.
Bsn.
Hn.
C Tpt.
Tbn.
Tba.
Timp.
Cym.
Vln. I
Vln. II
Vla.
Vc.
Db.

21
Picc.
Fl.
Ob.
Cl.
Bsn.
Hn.
C Tpt.
Tbn.
Tba.
Timp.
Cym.
Vln. I
Vln. II
Vla.
Vc.
Db.

26
Picc.
Fl.
Ob.
Cl.
Bsn.
Hn.
C Tpt.
Tbn.
Tba.
Timp.
Cym.
Vln. I
Vln. II
Vla.
Vc.
Db.

31
Picc.
Fl.
Ob.
Cl.
Bsn.
Hn.
C Tpt.
Tbn.
Tba.
Timp.
Cym.
Vln. I
Vln. II
Vla.
Vc.
Db.

36
Picc.
Fl.
Ob.
Cl.
Bsn.
Hn.
C Tpt.
Tbn.
Tba.
Timp.
Cym.
Vln. I
Vln. II
Vla.
Vc.
Db.

41
Picc.
Fl.
Ob.
Cl.
Bsn.
Hn.
C Tpt.
Tbn.
Tba.
Timp.
Cym.
Vln. I
Vln. II
Vla.
Vc.
Db.

46
Picc.
Fl.
Ob.
Cl.
Bsn.
Hn.
C Tpt.
Tbn.
Tba.
Timp.
Cym.
Vln. I
Vln. II
Vla.
Vc.
Db.

51
Picc.
Fl.
Ob.
Cl.
Bsn.
Hn.
C Tpt.
Tbn.
Tba.
Timp.
Cym.
Vln. I
Vln. II
Vla.
Vc.
Db.

56
Picc.
Fl.
Ob.
Cl.
Bsn.
Hn.
C Tpt.
Tbn.
Tba.
Timp.
Cym.
Vln. I
Vln. II
Vla.
Vc.
Db.

61
Picc.
Fl.
Ob.
Cl.
Bsn.
Hn.
C Tpt.
Tbn.
Tba.
Timp.
Cym.
Vln. I
Vln. II
Vla.
Vc.
Db.

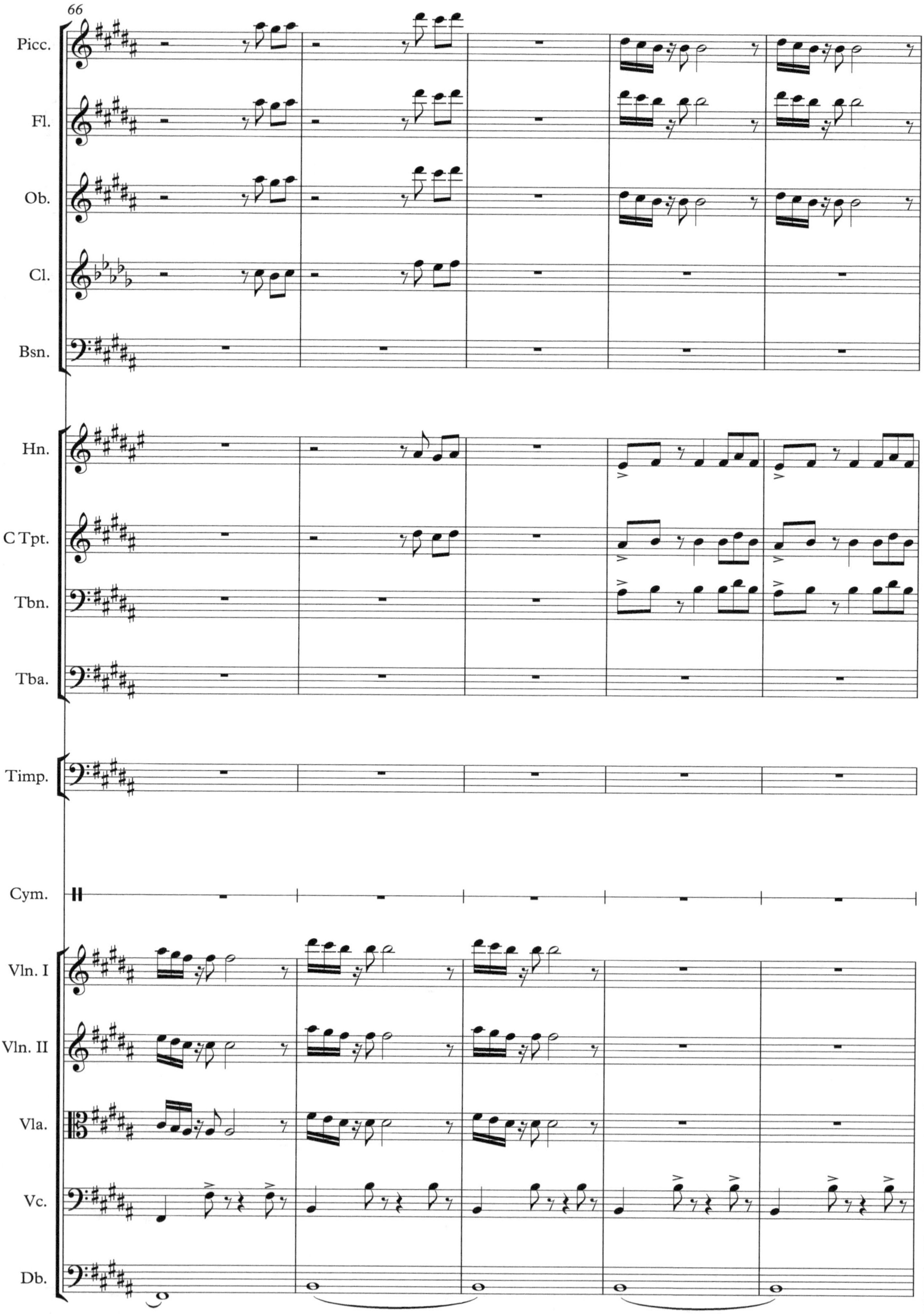
66
Picc.
Fl.
Ob.
Cl.
Bsn.
Hn.
C Tpt.
Tbn.
Tba.
Timp.
Cym.
Vln. I
Vln. II
Vla.
Vc.
Db.

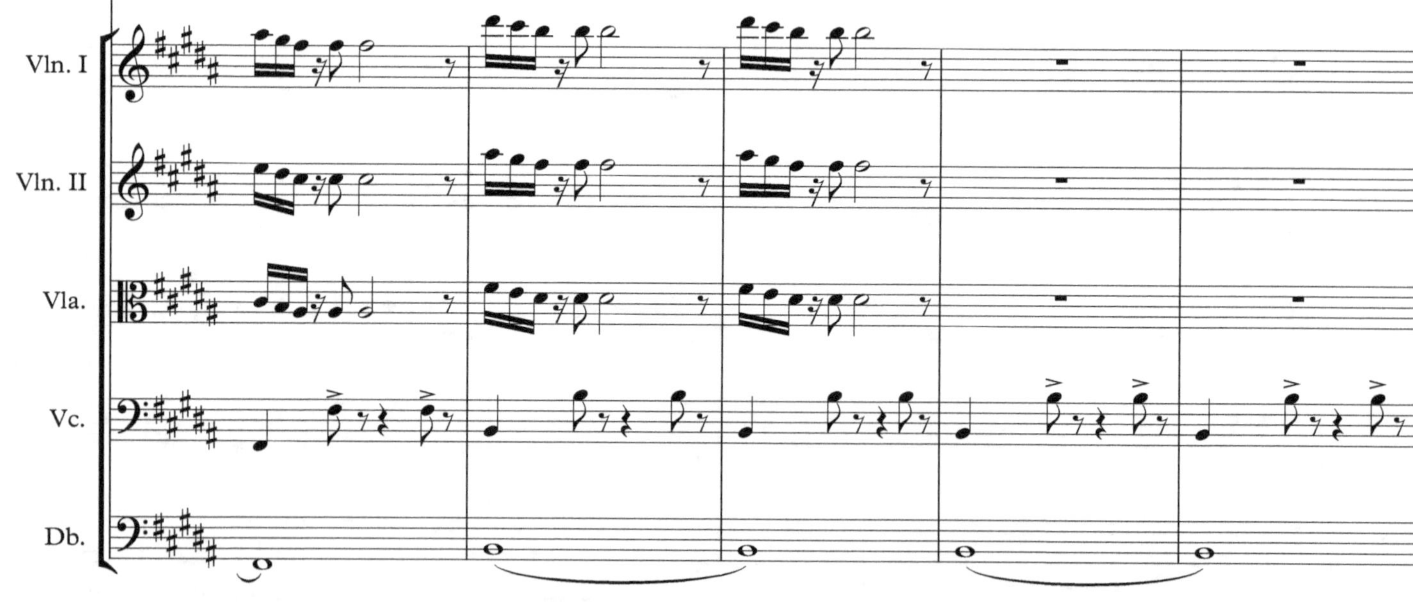

71
Picc.
Fl.
Ob.
Cl.
Bsn.
Hn.
C Tpt.
Tbn.
Tba.
Timp.
Cym.
Vln. I
Vln. II
Vla.
Vc.
Db.

75
Picc.
Fl.
Ob.
Cl.
Bsn.
Hn.
C Tpt.
Tbn.
Tba.
Timp.
Cym.
Vln. I
Vln. II
Vla.
Vc.
Db.

80
Picc.
Fl.
Ob.
Cl.
Bsn.
Hn.
C Tpt.
Tbn.
Tba.
Timp.
Cym.
Vln. I
Vln. II
Vla.
Vc.
Db.

85
Picc.
Fl.
Ob.
Cl.
Bsn.
Hn.
C Tpt.
Tbn.
Tba.
Timp.
Cym.
Vln. I
Vln. II
Vla.
Vc.
Db.

90
rall.
Picc.
Fl.
Ob.
Cl.
Bsn.
Hn.
C Tpt.
Tbn.
Tba.
Timp.
rall.
Cym.
Vln. I
Vln. II
Vla.
Vc.
Db.

96
Picc.
Fl.
Ob.
Cl.
Bsn.
Hn.
C Tpt.
Tbn.
Tba.
Timp.
Cym.
Vln. I
Vln. II
Vla.
Vc.
Db.

102
Picc.
Fl.
Ob.
Cl.
Bsn.
Hn.
C Tpt.
Tbn.
Tba.
Timp.
Cym.
Vln. I
Vln. II
Vla.
Vc.
Db.

ACT I

Scene III – Ambrogio and a Deal is Struck

The darkness is complete around the spotlight but then a red light starts to rise to reveal the cavern walls and the spotlight fades to leave Daethon afraid in a red light in the centre of the cave. On his knees he begs for succour and cries out for someone to aid him. Then from the shadows all around the Vampires arrive, tall, mean-spirited in their dancing and yet filled with a grace and elegance in their jumps and turns. Then with a blast the Darklord Ambrogio appears at the rear of the cave, approaching Daethon. Ambrogio dances around the helpless Daethon and shows him an image of Prince Arundel in a ghostly light. Daethon reaches for it but as quick as it appears Ambrogio whips it away. Daethon returns to his knees and begs Ambrogio to give him the power to win Arundel's heart. Ambrogio agrees and offers Daethon 100 years of joy with Arundel before Daethon must return to the cave and serve Ambrogio as one of his Vampires for all eternity. Daethon agrees and Ambrogio bites his neck, drinks his blood and takes his life, making him the undead. Daethon falls and then rises again; he is taken by the vampires and dressed in raiment and before the end of the scene they all dance to celebrate Daethon's turning, his power, his beauty and his new grace. The Vampires leave and Ambrogio sends Daethon off with his new power. Ambrogio is left alone in the cave to contemplate his deal when suddenly a ghostly pale blue light rises in a corner of the cave. Ambrogio turns to see Gullveig the Harpy, his ancient love and yet the most powerful threat to his power. With Gullveig come the ghostly Spirits who serve her, each pale and white except for their red beating hearts. Ambrogio and Gullveig play a game of cat and mouse on the stage, ever coming close to kiss then tricking the other, showing their eternal passionate conflict. Gullveig shows her power at the end and forces Ambrogio to his knees but then he fights free and darts to one of the Spirits and rips out its heart, holding it aloft. The Spirit falls to the floor dead and Ambrogio marches off stage triumphantly holding the heart on high, as the scene closes with Gullveig, beset with grief, collapsing over the body of her lost Spirit as the other Spirits flee through the opposite stage entrance to that which Ambrogio left through.

Choreography, Costume and Set Notes

- Ambrogio is tall and dressed in red and black, with a red-lined black cape, black eyes with contacts that mean he has no iris visible; the Vampires, all male, are all in black but with blood on their lips/chins and pale white faces; they are however very much vibrant proud dancers; they are slightly comic as Vampires but equally impressive, so the costumes are to be very fine and elegant.

- The Spirits, all female, dance en pointe, they flow and ebb on the stage, in long flowing white garments which are almost translucent; Gullveig is dressed in white also, but with light blue raiment over the top and a diamond tiara; all the Spirits have their hair long, but Gullveig's hair is up in an elaborate arrangement. Each Spirit has beneath their costume a vascular costume with blood vessels everywhere, visible through the overgarment. In the centre of the overgarment there is a hole over the heart and for each a satin red heart is visible (held securely in place by Velcro); the hearts need to be realistic not like figurative valentine hearts. They are supposed to be a grotesque aspect of the beautiful spirits and of course they represent the lifeforce of the Spirits.

- In Bar 19 Ambrogio arrives; in Bars 27 to 34 Ambrogio ignores Daethon's pleas and walks proudly amongst the dancing Vampires who mock Daethon with their dance; in Bars 35 to 42 Daethon finds more confidence and stands more proudly; in Bars 43 to 50 Ambrogio takes pity on Daethon and in Bars 51 to 58 Ambrogio shows him the leaps and bounds of his Vampires, asking him if he would consent to the deal. Deathon agrees and is suddenly held by the Vampires in Bars 59 to 64 before in Bar 65 Ambrogio bites Daethon and drops him seemingly dead to the floor in a white spotlight in centre stage before all retreat, leaving him alone to start to slowly move and come back to life in Bars 67 to 80. In Bars 81 to 92 Daethon arises with his new powers and as he stretches his limbs and steadily discovers his new strength he is dressed in his new raiment by the Vampires; Daethon's servant attire is removed and a brilliant blue cloak covers him to reveal a sparkling blue costume (which of course the dancer would simply already have been wearing concealed under the peasant clothing).

- In Bars 93 to 104 Daethon dances with glee with the Vampires as Ambrogio looks on with amusement and the dance is very athletic for Daethon is discovering his new powers.

- Finally Daethon and all the Vampires leave in Bar 104 to leave Ambrogio alone who dances a sombre solo; Gullveig and the Spirits then appear following the pale blue light in Bar 121.

❧ They dance together in what appears to be love but then in Bars 153 to 168 Gullveig forces Ambrogio to his knees and walks around him in captivity with her magic as the Spirits dance cruelly; in Bars 169 to 184 he steadily struggles as they dance and then breaks free at last in Bar 185 to Gullveig's shock; the Spirits dance chaotically as Gullveig falls to her knees begging for mercy and Ambrogio stalks powerfully towards her. Then in Bar 196 he grabs a passing Spirit and in Bar 198 he rips the heart from the Spirit and drops her dead to the floor; Gullveig is left wailing in sorrow on the floor for the last two bars as Ambrogio walks off stage to the last dying chord.

♪ = 135
Piccolo
Flute
Oboe
Horn in F
Trumpet in B♭
Trombone
Timpani
Cymbals
Harp
Choir
♪ = 135
Violin I
Violin II
Viola
Violoncello
Double Bass

6
Picc.
Fl.
Ob.
Hn.
Tpt.
Tbn.
Timp.
Cym.
Hp.
Choir
Vln. I
Vln. II
Vla.
Vc.
Db.

11
Picc.
Fl.
Ob.
Hn.
Tpt.
Tbn.
Timp.
Cym.
Hp.
Choir
Vln. I
Vln. II
Vla.
Vc.
Db.

16
Picc.
Fl.
Ob.
Hn.
Tpt.
Tbn.
tr
Timp.
Cym.
Hp.
Choir
Vln. I
Vln. II
Vla.
Vc.
Db.

21

Picc.

Fl.

Ob.

Hn.

Tpt.

Tbn.

Timp.

Cym.

Hp.

Choir

Vln. I

Vln. II

Vla.

Vc.

Db.

26
Picc.
Fl.
Ob.
Hn.
Tpt.
Tbn.
Timp.
Cym.
Hp.
Choir
Vln. I
Vln. II
Vla.
Vc.
Db.

32
Picc.
Fl.
Ob.
Hn.
Tpt.
Tbn.
Timp.
Cym.
Hp.
Choir
Vln. I
Vln. II
Vla.
Vc.
Db.

38
Picc.
Fl.
Ob.
Hn.
Tpt.
Tbn.
Timp.
Cym.
Hp.
Choir
Vln. I
Vln. II
Vla.
Vc.
Db.

44

Picc.
Fl.
Ob.
Hn.
Tpt.
Tbn.
Timp.
Cym.
Hp.
Choir
Vln. I
Vln. II
Vla.
Vc.
Db.

49
Picc.
Fl.
Ob.
Hn.
Tpt.
Tbn.
Timp.
Cym.
Hp.
Choir
Vln. I
Vln. II
Vla.
Vc.
Db.

54
molto rall.
11
Picc.
Fl.
Ob.
Hn.
Tpt.
Tbn.
tr
Timp.
Cym.
Hp.
Choir
molto rall.
Vln. I
Vln. II
Vla.
Vc.
Db.

60
♩ = 90
Picc.
Fl.
Ob.
Hn.
Tpt.
Tbn.
(tr)
tr
Timp.
Cym.
Hp.
Choir
Vln. I
Vln. II
Vla.
Vc.
Db.

69
Picc.
Fl.
Ob.
Hn.
Tpt.
Tbn.
Timp.
Cym.
Hp.
Choir
Vln. I
Vln. II
Vla.
Vc.
Db.

74
Picc.
Fl.
Ob.
Hn.
Tpt.
Tbn.
Timp.
Cym.
Hp.
Choir
Vln. I
Vln. II
Vla.
Vc.
Db.

79
Picc.
Fl.
Ob.
Hn.
Tpt.
Tbn.
Timp.
Cym.
Hp.
Choir
Vln. I
Vln. II
Vla.
Vc.
Db.

84
Picc.
Fl.
Ob.
Hn.
Tpt.
Tbn.
Timp.
Cym.
Hp.
Choir
Vln. I
Vln. II
Vla.
Vc.
Db.

89

Picc.
Fl.
Ob.
Hn.
Tpt.
Tbn.
Timp.
Cym.
Hp.
Choir
Vln. I
Vln. II
Vla.
Vc.
Db.

94
Picc.
Fl.
Ob.
Hn.
Tpt.
Tbn.
Timp.
Cym.
Hp.
Choir
Vln. I
Vln. II
Vla.
Vc.
Db.

99

Picc.
Fl.
Ob.
Hn.
Tpt.
Tbn.
Timp.
Cym.
Hp.
Choir
Vln. I
Vln. II
Vla.
Vc.
Db.

104
♪ = 135
Picc.
Fl.
Ob.
Hn.
Tpt.
Tbn.
Timp.
Cym.
Hp.
Choir
♪ = 135
Vln. I
Vln. II
Vla.
Vc.
Db.
p

116

molto accel.

Picc.

Fl.

Ob.

Hn.

Tpt.

Tbn.

Timp.

Cym.

Hp.

Choir

molto accel.

Vln. I

Vln. II

Vla.

Vc.

Db.

127
Picc.
Fl.
Ob.
Hn.
Tpt.
Tbn.
Timp.
Cym.
Hp.
Choir
Vln. I
Vln. II
p
Vla.
Vc.
Db.

136
Picc.
Fl.
Ob.
Hn.
Tpt.
Tbn.
Timp.
Cym.
Hp.
Choir
Vln. I
Vln. II
Vla.
Vc.
Db.

145
♩. = 90
Picc.
Fl.
Ob.
Hn.
Tpt.
Tbn.
Timp.
Cym.
Hp.
Choir
♩. = 90
Vln. I
Vln. II
p
Vla.
Vc.
Db.

154
Picc.
Fl.
Ob.
Hn.
Tpt.
Tbn.
Timp.
Cym.
Hp.
Choir
Vln. I
Vln. II
Vla.
Vc.
Db.

163
Picc.
Fl.
Ob.
Hn.
Tpt.
Tbn.
Timp.
Cym.
Hp.
Choir
Vln. I
Vln. II
Vla.
Vc.
Db.

172
Picc.
Fl.
Ob.
Hn.
Tpt.
Tbn.
Timp.
Cym.
Hp.
Choir
Vln. I
Vln. II
Vla.
Vc.
Db.

180
Picc.
Fl.
Ob.
Hn.
Tpt.
Tbn.
tr
Timp.
Cym.
Hp.
Choir
Vln. I
Vln. II
Vla.
Vc.
Db.

188
Picc.
Fl.
Ob.
Hn.
Tpt.
Tbn.
Timp.
Cym.
Hp.
Choir
Vln. I
Vln. II
Vla.
Vc.
Db.

195
molto rall.
Picc.
Fl.
Ob.
Hn.
Tpt.
Tbn.
tr
Timp.
Cym.
Hp.
Choir
molto rall.
Vln. I
Vln. II
Vla.
Vc.
Db.

ACT I

Scene IV – Lorelle and the Witch

In the Garden of the palace Princess Lorelle and Prince Udolf are scheming, and the Princess Lorelle shows to him King Haelan's crown, which she stole from the Royal Chambers. She says to him that he should wear it and that together they should rule, but Prince Udolf is afraid and runs from the Garden in fear. The Princess wanders the Garden wondering, flitting from corner to corner until suddenly in a very dark corner amongst gnarled trees a hooded bent witch suddenly appears. She takes the crown and listens to the Princess' desires and in the end gives unto Lorelle a magical ring which will allow her consort, Prince Udolf, to pass for anyone he desires and to achieve all that she hopes for. In exchange the witch demands the first child that the two have together. Lorelle is beset by horror at the thought initially but then, seeing visions of Udolf crowned on the throne, she agrees. She hurries off with the ring leaving the witch alone in the Garden. The Garden melts away and the cloak falls to reveal the witch as Gullveig and she dances a wicked dance of joy before the scene ends now that she has begun her wicked plan to recover the heart stolen from her.

Choreography, Costume and Set Notes

- The scene begins with an elegant pas de deux to introduce the two characters together and then Lorelle starts to try to force the crown on Udolf from Bar 17. In Bar 32 Udolf thrusts the crown back at Lorelle and runs off stage in fear.

- Lorelle wanders and flits in her dance in the Garden until she meets the witch in Bar 49 and the future desires of the witch and the powers of the ring are conveyed through use of silhouettes behind the garden which the witch shows in Bars 57 to 64 to Lorelle.

- Lorelle is convinced and hurries off with the ring after first dancing in joy to have it, holding it aloft throughout a dance sequence; once Lorelle has left the stage by Bar 72 then the witch slowly walks forward and sheds her cloak to reveal herself as Gullveig in the same outfit as before in Bar 73; she then dances a dance of triumph to the end.

♩ = 75
Flute
Oboe
English Horn
Clarinet in B♭
Horn in F
Trumpet in C
Tuba
Timpani
Glockenspiel
Choir
♩ = 75
Violin I
Violin II
Viola
Violoncello
Double Bass

4
Fl.
Ob.
Eng. Hn.
Cl.
Hn.
C Tpt.
Tba.
Timp.
Glock.
Choir
Vln. I
Vln. II
Vla.
Vc.
Db.

8

Fl.

Ob.

Eng. Hn.

Cl.

Hn.

C Tpt.

Tba.

Timp.

Glock.

Choir

Vln. I

Vln. II

Vla.

Vc.

Db.

11
Fl.
Ob.
Eng. Hn.
Cl.
Hn.
C Tpt.
Tba.
Timp.
Glock.
Choir
Vln. I
Vln. II
Vla.
Vc.
Db.

14
Fl.
Ob.
Eng. Hn.
Cl.
Hn.
C Tpt.
Tba.
Timp.
Glock.
Choir
Vln. I
Vln. II
Vla.
Vc.
Db.

18
Fl.
Ob.
Eng. Hn.
Cl.
Hn.
C Tpt.
Tba.
Timp.
Glock.
Choir
Vln. I
Vln. II
Vla.
Vc.
Db.

22
Fl.
Ob.
Eng. Hn.
Cl.
Hn.
C Tpt.
Tba.
Timp.
Glock.
Choir
Vln. I
Vln. II
Vla.
Vc.
Db.

26

Fl.

Ob.

Eng. Hn.

Cl.

Hn.

C Tpt.

Tba.

Timp.

Glock.

Choir

Vln. I

Vln. II

Vla.

Vc.

Db.

30
Fl.
Ob.
Eng. Hn.
Cl.
Hn.
C Tpt.
Tba.
Timp.
Glock.
Choir
Vln. I
Vln. II
Vla.
Vc.
Db.

34
Fl.
Ob.
Eng. Hn.
Cl.
Hn.
C Tpt.
Tba.
Timp.
Glock.
Choir
Vln. I
Vln. II
Vla.
Vc.
Db.

38
Fl.
Ob.
Eng. Hn.
Cl.
Hn.
C Tpt.
Tba.
Timp.
Glock.
Choir
Vln. I
Vln. II
Vla.
Vc.
Db.

42
Fl.
Ob.
Eng. Hn.
Cl.
Hn.
C Tpt.
Tba.
Timp.
Glock.
Choir
Vln. I
Vln. II
Vla.
Vc.
Db.

46
Fl.
Ob.
Eng. Hn.
Cl.
Hn.
C Tpt.
Tba.
Timp.
Glock.
Choir
Vln. I
Vln. II
Vla.
Vc.
Db.

50

Fl.

Ob.

Eng. Hn.

Cl.

Hn.

C Tpt.

Tba.

Timp.

Glock.

Choir

Vln. I

Vln. II

Vla.

Vc.

Db.

54

Fl.
Ob.
Eng. Hn.
Cl.
Hn.
C Tpt.
Tba.
Timp.
Glock.
Choir
Vln. I
Vln. II
Vla.
Vc.
Db.

58
Fl.
Ob.
Eng. Hn.
Cl.
Hn.
C Tpt.
Tba.
Timp.
Glock.
Choir
Vln. I
Vln. II
Vla.
Vc.
Db.

62
Fl.
Ob.
Eng. Hn.
Cl.
Hn.
C Tpt.
Tba.
Timp.
Glock.
Choir
Vln. I
Vln. II
Vla.
Vc.
Db.

66
Fl.
Ob.
Eng. Hn.
Cl.
Hn.
C Tpt.
Tba.
Timp.
Glock.
Choir
Vln. I
Vln. II
Vla.
Vc.
Db.

70
Fl.
Ob.
Eng. Hn.
Cl.
Hn.
C Tpt.
Tba.
Timp.
Glock.
Choir
Vln. I
Vln. II
Vla.
Vc.
Db.

74
Fl.
Ob.
Eng. Hn.
Cl.
Hn.
C Tpt.
Tba.
Timp.
Glock.
Choir
Vln. I
Vln. II
Vla.
Vc.
Db.

74
Fl.
Ob.
Eng. Hn.
Cl.
Hn.
C Tpt.
Tba.
Timp.
Glock.
Choir
Vln. I
Vln. II
Vla.
Vc.
Db.

rall.
77
Fl.
Ob.
Eng. Hn.
Cl.
Hn.
C Tpt.
Tba.
Timp.
tr
Glock.
Choir
rall.
Vln. I
Vln. II
Vla.
Vc.
Db.

ACT I

Scene V – The Midsummer Ball

The Prince is at court, the King is away, and the Nobles and their ladies have gathered for the Midsummer Ball. All dance together and then Daethon, dressed in his finery enters and all stop to see him. All are amazed by the new stranger and honour and acknowledge him, dancing vigorously together. The Prince finally arrives and enters the Great Hall; with a wave of his hand the Nobles and Ladies, all compelled, stop dancing, bow low and exit bowing, much to Arundel's surprise. Then from the far side of the hall he sees Daethon and is at once captivated. Daethon approaches and the two of them commence a steady duet together coming close and apart and close and apart, their affection evident and Daethon's beauty and grace equal now to the Prince's. They dance with greater and greater synchrony and their dance takes them into the Garden where the two finally embrace, kiss and enjoin in their love. At last the scene ends with Daethon lain in the Prince's arms, the Prince on his knees, kissing Daethon, both out of breath but filled with love as the Act finishes.

Choreography, Costume and Set Notes

- The scene begins in an elegant ballroom with the Nobles dancing the waltz and Daethon enters in Bar 21 dressed in finery for the ball.
- Prince Arundel enters in Bar 100 and in Bars 101 to 106 the nobles and ladies all depart to leave Daethon and Arundel alone.
- At Bar 159 Daethon grabs Arundel's hand and they run together to the Garden where in Bar 175 they finally embrace and kiss deeply; they dance together joyfully to the end of the scene with Daethon lain in the Prince's arms for the final rallentando from Bar 199.

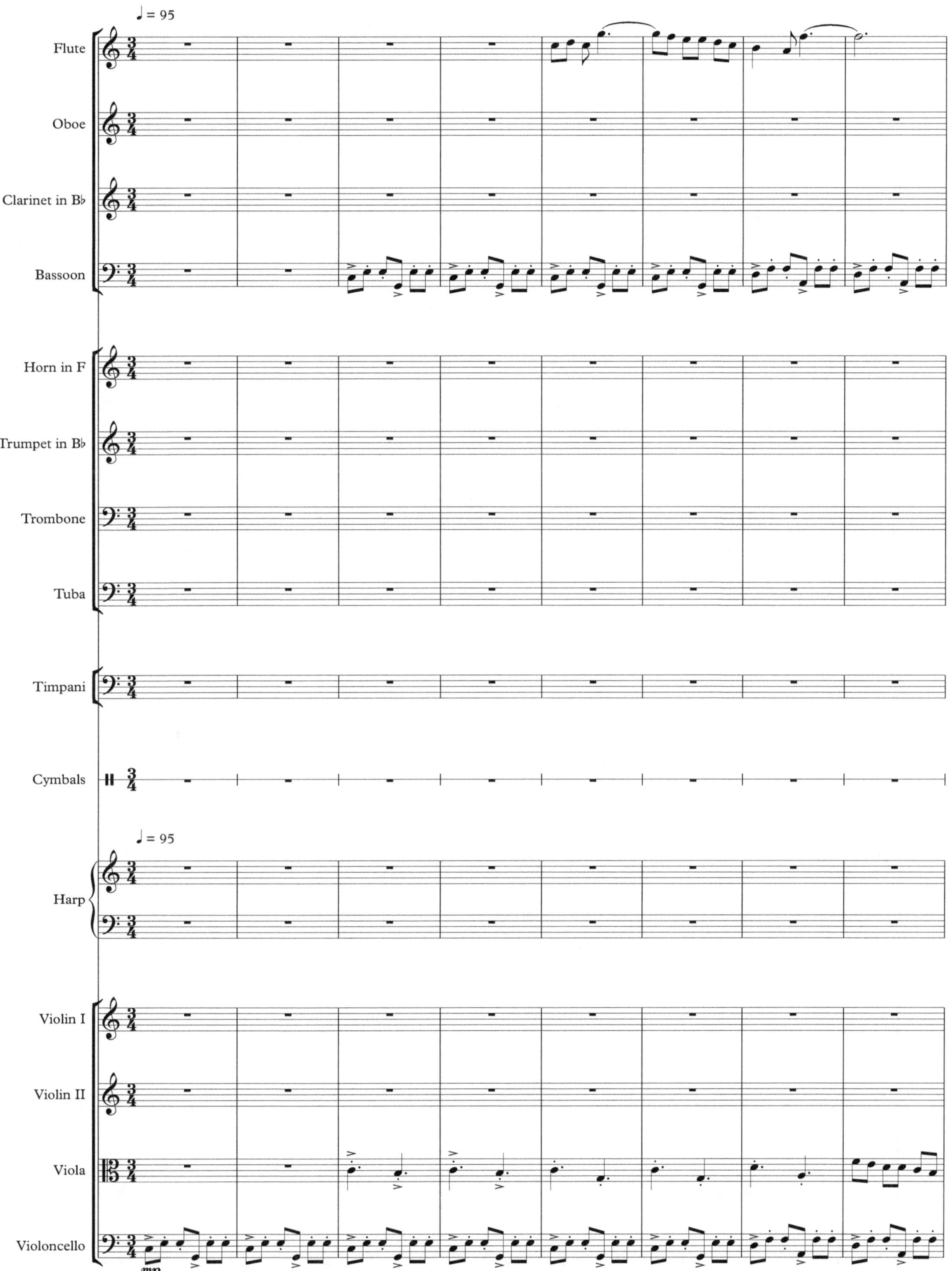

♩ = 95
Flute
Oboe
Clarinet in B♭
Bassoon
Horn in F
Trumpet in B♭
Trombone
Tuba
Timpani
Cymbals
♩ = 95
Harp
Violin I
Violin II
Viola
Violoncello
mp

9
Fl.
Ob.
Cl.
Bsn.
Hn.
Tpt.
Tbn.
Tba.
Timp.
Cym.
Hp.
Vln. I
Vln. II
Vla.
Vc.

18

Fl.

Ob.

Cl.

Bsn.

Hn.

Tpt.

Tbn.

Tba.

Timp.

Cym.

Hp.

Vln. I

Vln. II

Vla.

Vc.

26
Fl.
Ob.
Cl.
Bsn.
Hn.
Tpt.
Tbn.
Tba.
Timp.
Cym.
Hp.
Vln. I
Vln. II
Vla.
Vc.

35
Fl.
Ob.
Cl.
Bsn.
Hn.
Tpt.
Tbn.
Tba.
Timp.
Cym.
Hp.
Vln. I
Vln. II
Vla.
Vc.

44
Fl.
Ob.
Cl.
Bsn.
Hn.
Tpt.
Tbn.
Tba.
Timp.
Cym.
Hp.
Vln. I
Vln. II
Vla.
Vc.

53
Fl.
Ob.
Cl.
Bsn.
Hn.
Tpt.
Tbn.
Tba.
Timp.
Cym.
Hp.
Vln. I
Vln. II
Vla.
Vc.

62
Fl.
Ob.
Cl.
Bsn.
Hn.
Tpt.
Tbn.
Tba.
Timp.
Cym.
Hp.
Vln. I
Vln. II
Vla.
Vc.

71
Fl.
Ob.
Cl.
Bsn.
Hn.
Tpt.
Tbn.
Tba.
Timp.
Cym.
Hp.
Vln. I
Vln. II
Vla.
Vc.

80
Fl.
Ob.
Cl.
Bsn.
Hn.
Tpt.
Tbn.
Tba.
Timp.
Cym.
Hp.
Vln. I
Vln. II
Vla.
Vc.

89

Fl.
Ob.
Cl.
Bsn.
Hn.
Tpt.
Tbn.
Tba.
Timp.
Cym.
Hp.
Vln. I
Vln. II
Vla.
Vc.

97
molto rall.
♩= 105
poco accel.
Fl.
Ob.
Cl.
Bsn.
Hn.
Tpt.
Tbn.
Tba.
Timp.
Cym.
♩= 105
molto rall.
poco accel.
Hp.
Vln. I
Vln. II
tremolo
nat.
Vla.
nat.
Vc.
nat.

108
Fl.
Ob.
Cl.
Bsn.
Hn.
Tpt.
Tbn.
Tba.
Timp.
Cym.
Hp.
Vln. I
Vln. II
Vla.
Vc.
mp
pp

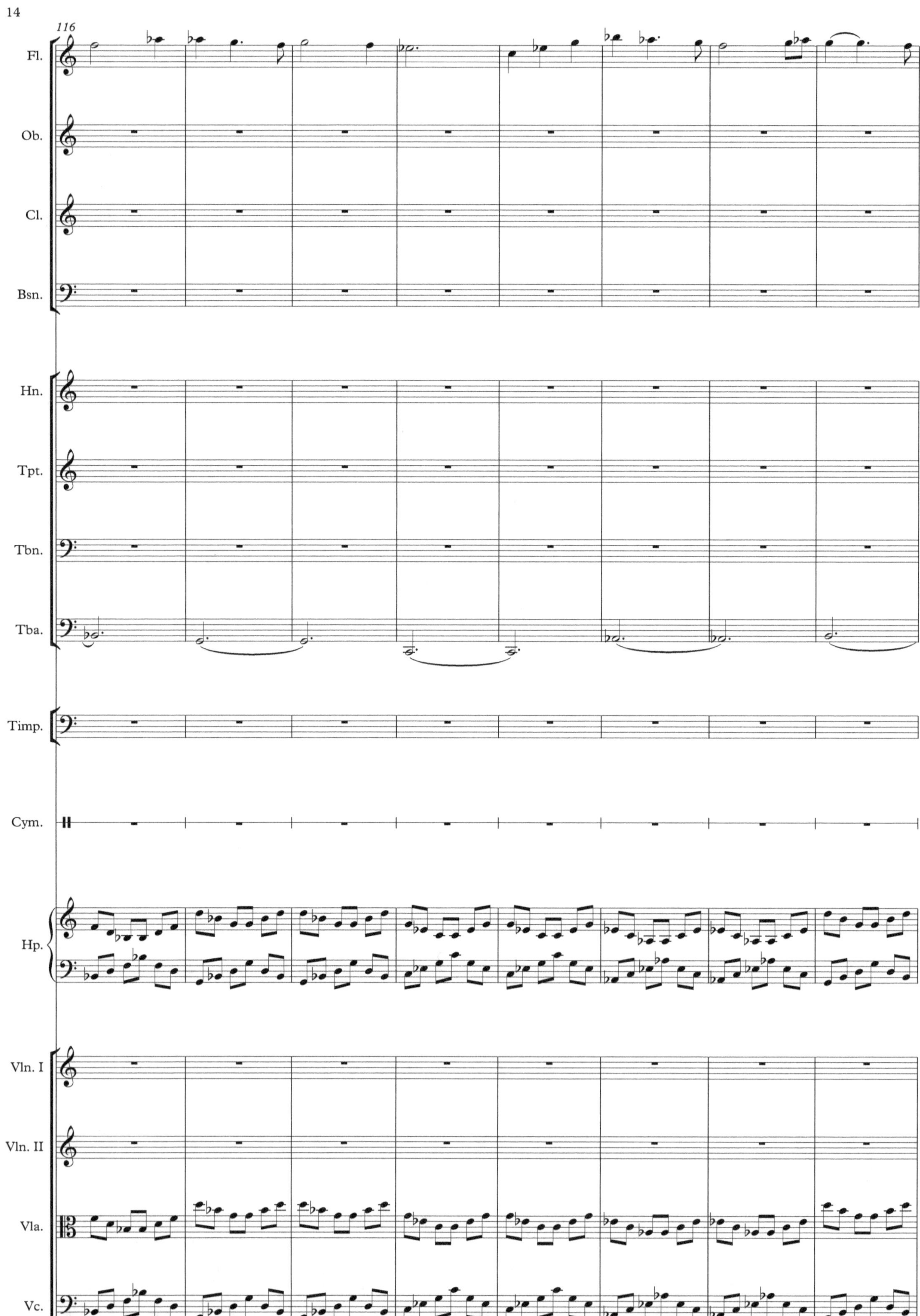
116
Fl.
Ob.
Cl.
Bsn.
Hn.
Tpt.
Tbn.
Tba.
Timp.
Cym.
Hp.
Vln. I
Vln. II
Vla.
Vc.

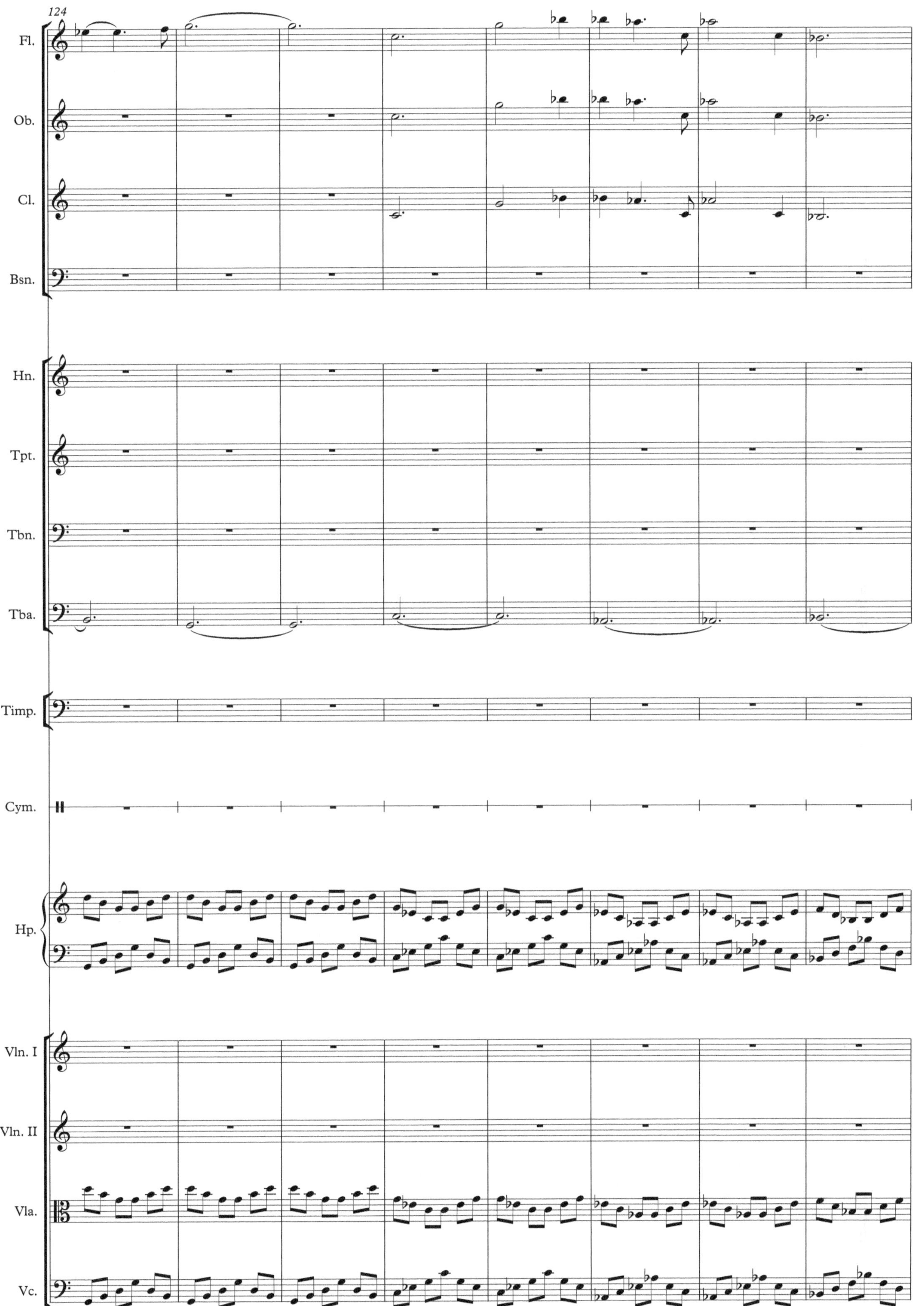
124
Fl.
Ob.
Cl.
Bsn.
Hn.
Tpt.
Tbn.
Tba.
Timp.
Cym.
Hp.
Vln. I
Vln. II
Vla.
Vc.

132
Fl.
Ob.
Cl.
Bsn.
Hn.
Tpt.
Tbn.
Tba.
Timp.
Cym.
Hp.
Vln. I
Vln. II
Vla.
Vc.

140
Fl.
Ob.
Cl.
Bsn.
Hn.
Tpt.
Tbn.
Tba.
Timp.
Cym.
Hp.
Vln. I
Vln. II
Vla.
Vc.
f

148
Fl.
Ob.
Cl.
Bsn.
Hn.
Tpt.
Tbn.
Tba.
Timp.
Cym.
Hp.
Vln. I
Vln. II
Vla.
Vc.

156
Fl.
Ob.
Cl.
Bsn.
Hn.
mf
Tpt.
Tbn.
Tba.
f
Timp.
Cym.
Hp.
Vln. I
Vln. II
Vla.
Vc.

164
Fl.
Ob.
Cl.
Bsn.
Hn.
Tpt.
Tbn.
Tba.
Timp.
Cym.
Hp.
Vln. I
p
Vln. II
Vla.
Vc.

173
Fl.
Ob.
Cl.
Bsn.
Hn.
Tpt.
Tbn.
Tba.
Timp.
Cym.
Hp.
Vln. I
Vln. II
Vla.
Vc.
mp
p
p

181
Fl.
Ob.
Cl.
Bsn.
Hn.
Tpt.
Tbn.
Tba.
Timp.
Cym.
Hp.
Vln. I
Vln. II
Vla.
Vc.

189
Fl.
Ob.
Cl.
Bsn.
Hn.
Tpt.
Tbn.
Tba.
Timp.
Cym.
Hp.
Vln. I
Vln. II
Vla.
Vc.
mp
pp
pp
pp
pp

197
rall.
Fl.
Ob.
Cl.
Bsn.
Hn.
Tpt.
Tbn.
Tba.
Timp.
Cym.
rall.
Hp.
Vln. I
Vln. II
Vla.
Vc.

202
Fl.
Ob.
Cl.
Bsn.
Hn.
Tpt.
Tbn.
Tba.
Timp.
Cym.
Hp.
Vln. I
Vln. II
Vla.
Vc.
ppp

ACT II

ACT II

Scene I – The Ring

Princess Lorelle is in her chambers admiring the ring that the Harpy gave her and a lady in waiting comes a-knocking. It is Prince Udolf and the Princess quickly has him ushered in and dismisses the girl. Now the scheming sister begins her plotting and shows Udolf the ring and tells him of Gullveig's magic. Udolf is initially uncertain and they argue, but he is convinced in the end as Lorelle beguiles him. She gets him to put on the ring and in an instant he is transformed into the very likeness of Daethon. Lorelle shows him this by looking into a mirror, and in the mirror he appears to be Daethon. In glee they dance together at the coming together of their plotting as the scene ends.

Choreography, Costume and Set Notes

- Udolf enters at Bar 25 and from Bar 33 they argue; the dance must involve them coming together to dance and then Udolf pushing Lorelle aside in disgust whenever she offers the ring.

- In Bar 41 Lorelle gains the upper hand as her theme begins to play and then in Bar 65 Udolf finally puts on the ring and in incredulity approaches the mirror to see Daethon reflected back at him; to achieve this the mirror in centre stage actually is just glass and Daethon is behind it to give the impression of a reflection. Some fun can be had here with mimicked movements between the two in the mirror.

- From Bar 73 to the end, the two dance a cruel and evil pas de deux with the ring held high in joyous triumph at the plot they have hatched.

♩ = 65
Flute
Oboe
mp
Clarinet in B♭
Bassoon
Horn in F
Trumpet in C
Trombone
Tuba
Timpani
Choir
♩ = 65
Violin I
Violin II
Viola
Violoncello
Double Bass

9
Fl.
Ob.
Cl.
Bsn.
Hn.
C Tpt.
Tbn.
Tba.
Timp.
p
Choir
p
Vln. I
Vln. II
Vla.
Vc.
Db.

17

Fl.
Ob.
Cl.
Bsn.
Hn.
C Tpt.
Tbn.
Tba.
Timp.
Choir
Vln. I
Vln. II
Vla.
Vc.
Db.

24
Fl.
Ob.
Cl.
Bsn.
Hn.
C Tpt.
Tbn.
Tba.
Timp.
Choir
Vln. I
Vln. II
Vla.
Vc.
Db.

30

Fl.

Ob.

Cl.

Bsn.

Hn.

C Tpt.

Tbn.

Tba.

Timp.

Choir

Vln. I

Vln. II

Vla.

Vc.

Db.

35
Fl.
Ob.
Cl.
Bsn.
Hn.
C Tpt.
Tbn.
Tba.
Timp.
Choir
Vln. I
Vln. II
Vla.
Vc.
Db.

40
Fl.
Ob.
Cl.
Bsn.
Hn.
C Tpt.
Tbn.
Tba.
Timp.
Choir
mp
Vln. I
Vln. II
Vla.
Vc.
Db.

47
Fl.
Ob.
Cl.
Bsn.
Hn.
C Tpt.
Tbn.
Tba.
Timp.
mf
Choir
mf
Vln. I
Vln. II
Vla.
Vc.
Db.

55
Fl.
Ob.
Cl.
Bsn.
Hn.
C Tpt.
Tbn.
Tba.
Timp.
Choir
Vln. I
Vln. II
Vla.
Vc.
Db.

62
Fl.
Ob.
Cl.
Bsn.
Hn.
C Tpt.
Tbn.
Tba.
tr
Timp.
Choir
Vln. I
Vln. II
p
Vla.
p
Vc.
p
Db.
p

69
Fl.
Ob.
Cl.
Bsn.
Hn.
C Tpt.
Tbn.
Tba.
Timp.
mp
Choir
mp
Vln. I
Vln. II
Vla.
Vc.
Db.

77
rall.
Fl.
Ob.
Cl.
Bsn.
Hn.
C Tpt.
Tbn.
Tba.
Timp.
Choir
rall.
Vln. I
Vln. II
Vla.
Vc.
Db.

ACT II

Scene II – Murder

Prince Udolf comes to the Garden wearing the ring which makes him appear as Daethon; he dances alone, initially tentatively, but then with more exuberance before suddenly Arundel arrives and he hides behind a bush. Udolf's courage grows and he nervously approaches. Arundel however is completely fooled and believing it is Daethon, the two of them dance together and Arundel expresses his love with greater and greater affection. Udolf dances aloofly and then as Arundel loses himself in a solo, Udolf slowly pulls a dagger from his robes and approaches him, only to stab him at the climax. Arundel in shock drops to the ground dying and Udolf steps back in horror, unable now to believe what he has done, dropping the knife in horror. Arundel dies, and as shouts come from afar, Udolf panics and flees. The Nobles come running into the Garden to find Arundel dead and quickly make chase after the man they believe to be Daethon. Back in the Garden Arundel's body lies alone, a pale light forms around it and we see the real Daethon come to the corpse and then weep in the most terrible grief at the loss; at the last he flees in horror and sadness from the scene as the lights go down on Arundel.

Choreography, Costume and Set Notes

- Wearing the ring, Udolf of course must look like Daethon, so is attired in blue to resemble Daethon and Arundel is again in white.

- When the dark and murderous music first starts the stage is black then filled with a dark red light of blood before the pale light grows and Udolf enters in Bar 11. The initial solo then starts in Bar 15.

- In Bars 23 to 54 the dance grows more exuberant with more jumps before in Bar 55 the music suddenly goes quiet and Arundel enters the Garden; just before this moment Udolf must clearly see him coming and thus duck behind a bush.

- In Bar 87 Udolf finally reveals himself having watched Arundel doing a romantic solo alone for a while.

- The two of them dance together more and more impressively and joyously up to Bar 119 where, Arundel continuing to dance happily on his own, Udolf separates away, draws his dagger and slowly approaches the dancing Arundel from behind only to stab him in Bar 131. Arundel looks at the man he believes to be Daethon in horror before finally falling dead in Bar 133.

- Udolf drops the dagger in horror in Bar 135 with the pool of blood forming on the floor and runs; just as he exits the stage some of the Nobles come running on stage from the opposite side and find the body. They are in shock but then chase after the assailant. The chase can be shown using a dropped curtain and lighting to show the nobles pursuing Udolf still wearing the ring.

- The chase scene ends in Bar 157 and now the separating curtain that was front-lit suddenly becomes back-lit again to reveal Arundel's body in a bright white spotlight centre-stage where it was before. The real Daethon now approaches and falls in tears and horror at the body, lifting his upper body up and crying profusely. From Bar 182 Daethon then slowly stands and steels himself to the awful loss before slowly walking backwards away from the body, still filled with sadness but also a growing anger for revenge as he finally is just off stage as the scene ends and the lights go down.

♩ = 75
Piccolo
Flute
Clarinet in B♭
Bassoon
Trumpet in C
Trombone
Tuba
Timpani
Cymbals
Choir
♩ = 75
Violin I
Violin II
Viola
Violoncello
Double Bass

9
Picc.
Fl.
Cl.
Bsn.
C Tpt.
Tbn.
Tba.
Timp.
Cym.
Choir
Vln. I
Vln. II
Vla.
Vc.
Db.

16

Picc.

Fl.

Cl.

Bsn.

C Tpt.

Tbn.

Tba.

Timp.

Cym.

Choir

Vln. I

Vln. II

Vla.

Vc.

Db.

21
Picc.
Fl.
Cl.
Bsn.
C Tpt.
Tbn.
Tba.
Timp.
Cym.
Choir
Vln. I
Vln. II
Vla.
Vc.
Db.

28
Picc.
Fl.
Cl.
Bsn.
C Tpt.
Tbn.
Tba.
Timp.
Cym.
Choir
Vln. I
Vln. II
Vla.
Vc.
Db.

35
Picc.
Fl.
Cl.
Bsn.
C Tpt.
Tbn.
Tba.
Timp.
Cym.
Choir
Vln. I
Vln. II
Vla.
Vc.
Db.

41
Picc.
Fl.
Cl.
Bsn.
C Tpt.
Tbn.
Tba.
Timp.
Cym.
Choir
Vln. I
Vln. II
Vla.
Vc.
Db.

48
rall.
♩ = 100
accel.
Picc.
Fl.
Cl.
Bsn.
C Tpt.
Tbn.
Tba.
Timp.
Cym.
Choir
rall.
♩ = 100
accel.
Vln. I
pp
Vln. II
Vla.
pp
Vc.
pp
Db.

58
Picc.
Fl.
Cl.
Bsn.
C Tpt.
Tbn.
Tba.
Timp.
Cym.
Choir
Vln. I
Vln. II
Vla.
Vc.
Db.
p
p
p
pp
pp

72
Picc.
Fl.
Cl.
Bsn.
C Tpt.
Tbn.
Tba.
Timp.
Cym.
Choir
Vln. I
Vln. II
Vla.
Vc.
Db.

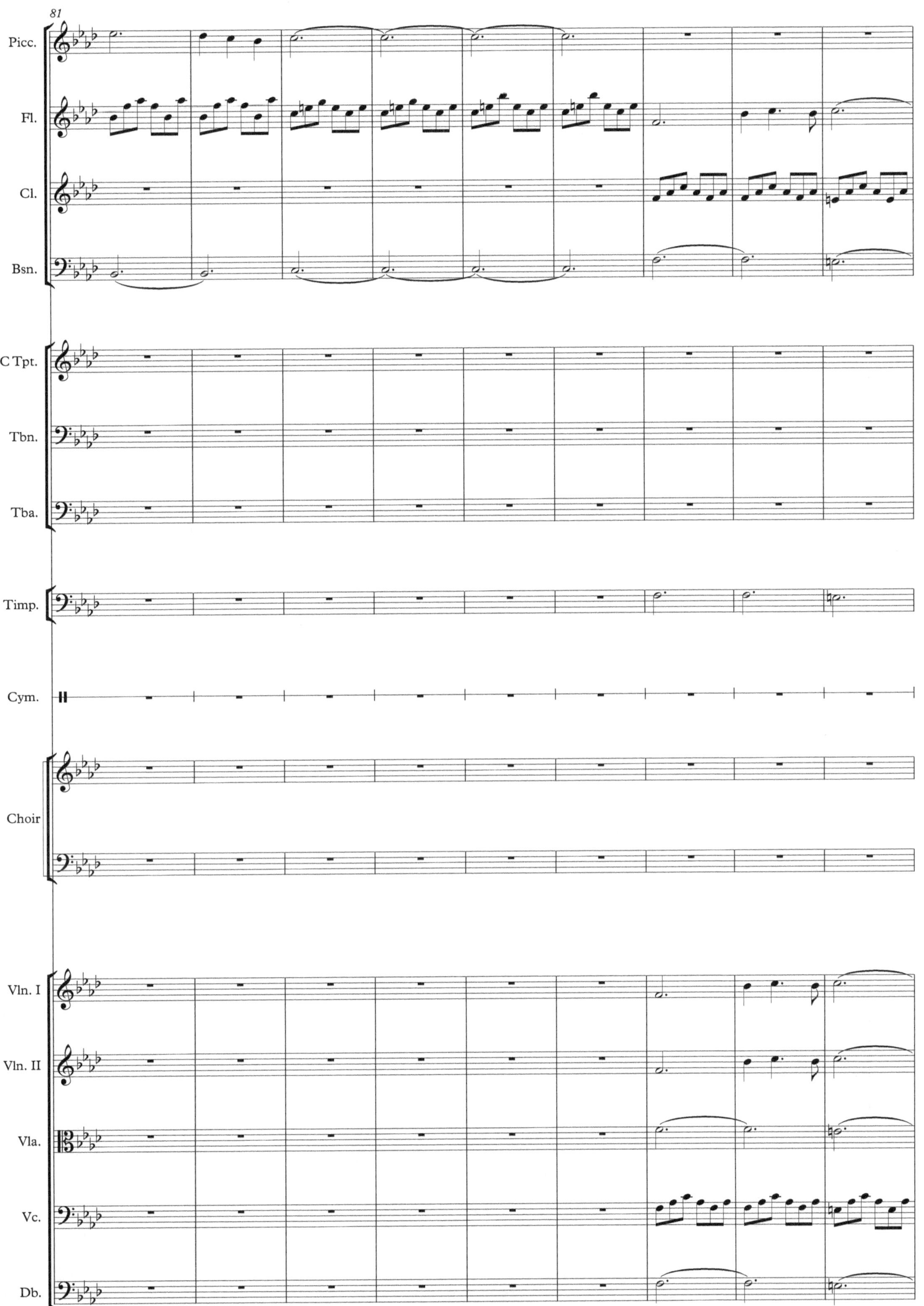
81
Picc.
Fl.
Cl.
Bsn.
C Tpt.
Tbn.
Tba.
Timp.
Cym.
Choir
Vln. I
Vln. II
Vla.
Vc.
Db.

90
Picc.
Fl.
Cl.
Bsn.
C Tpt.
Tbn.
Tba.
Timp.
Cym.
Choir
Vln. I
Vln. II
Vla.
Vc.
Db.

99

Picc.

Fl.

Cl.

Bsn.

C Tpt.

Tbn.

Tba.

Timp.

Cym.

Choir

Vln. I

Vln. II

Vla.

Vc.

Db.

108
Picc.
Fl.
Cl.
Bsn.
C Tpt.
Tbn.
Tba.
Timp.
Cym.
Choir
Vln. I
Vln. II
Vla.
Vc.
Db.

117
Picc.
Fl.
Cl.
Bsn.
C Tpt.
Tbn.
Tba.
Timp.
Cym.
Choir
Vln. I
Vln. II
Vla.
Vc.
Db.

126
♩ = 85
Picc.
Fl.
Cl.
Bsn.
C Tpt.
Tbn.
Tba.
tr
Timp.
Cym.
Choir
Vln. I
Vln. II
Vla.
Vc.
Db.
mf

137

Picc.

Fl.

Cl.

Bsn.

C Tpt.

Tbn.

Tba.

Timp.

Cym.

Choir

Vln. I

Vln. II

Vla.

Vc.

Db.

143
Picc.
Fl.
Cl.
Bsn.
C Tpt.
Tbn.
Tba.
Timp.
Cym.
f
Choir
Vln. I
Vln. II
Vla.
Vc.
Db.

149
Picc.
Fl.
Cl.
Bsn.
C Tpt.
Tbn.
Tba.
Timp.
Cym.
Choir
Vln. I
Vln. II
Vla.
Vc.
Db.

155
♩= 75
Picc.
Fl.
Cl.
Bsn.
C Tpt.
Tbn.
Tba.
Timp.
Cym.
Choir
Vln. I
Vln. II
Vla.
Vc.
Db.
tr
mp
p
♩= 75

169
Picc.
Fl.
Cl.
Bsn.
C Tpt.
Tbn.
Tba.
Timp.
Cym.
Choir
Vln. I
Vln. II
Vla.
Vc.
Db.

180
poco rall.
p
Picc.
Fl.
Cl.
Bsn.
C Tpt.
Tbn.
Tba.
Timp.
Cym.
Choir
poco rall.
Vln. I
tremolo
Vln. II
ppp
Vla.
Vc.
Db.

190

Picc.

Fl.

Cl.

Bsn.

C Tpt.

Tbn.

Tba.

Timp.

Cym.

Choir

Vln. I

Vln. II

Vla.

Vc.

Db.

ACT II

Scene III – A Marriage in Misery

A month has passed and King Haelan, still in misery, has presided over the wedding of the Princess Lorelle to Prince Udolf. The festivities are great but there is an air of sadness about the King that cannot be lifted despite the efforts of the Princess. She gives up and dances with glee with her new husband knowing that she will now rule the kingdom alongside him with Arundel dead. A hooded figure watches the festivities however and the Princess knows that her promise to Gullveig hangs over her. She must give up her first-born child to Gullveig in return for the ring she was granted. All of a sudden, the hooded figure reveals herself when Lorelle and Udolf are alone, showing herself to be the Harpy. She demands the return of the ring and Udolf and Lorelle return it terrified, but the Harpy then departs, and their confidence returns. They believe that they can carry on and now they need only wait until the passing of King Haelan and the land will be theirs.

Choreography, Costume and Set Notes

- The scene opens to the Great Hall with the King sat upon the throne deeply and obviously unhappy. Lorelle and Udolf, dressed in marriage finery (Lorelle in white and Udolf in gilt and red) encourage the Nobles and Ladies to dance and they do but Lorelle meanwhile goes to the king and tries to cheer him, holding his hand.

- By Bar 21 Lorelle gives up and takes the hand of Udolf to dance together anyway, whilst the King remains sat in misery.

- In Bar 37 the King gets up and with his guards leaves the throne room, no longer happy to partake in the festivities.

- From Bar 53 the lights centre on Lorelle and Udolf dancing and the other Nobles and Ladies dance off stage whilst the hooded figure who was previously merely standing in the corner watching now begins to circle the stage slowly.

- In a flash of dark blue light in Bar 61 the Harpy suddenly reveals herself, throwing off her hooded cloak and stepping up into a couru en pointe whilst in the blazing light; she wears a startling blue gown and a headdress of diamonds down her back; in the flash of light the four previously unlit braziers in the four corners of the stage burst into flames.

- The Harpy circles the two of them until Bar 76 when she then approaches and with outstretched hand demands the ring. At this moment the Spirits enter from all sides in their ghostly attire, showing again their beating hearts. Udolf gives up the ring in dread as Lorelle cowers and then the two of them cower in fear as Gullveig and the Spirits dance around them menacingly until Bar 100.

- The lights slowly lower and the braziers go out as Gullveig and all the Spirits slowly recede off stage by Bar 107; Udolf and Lorelle are left in a small pool of light from which they tentatively raise themselves before hugging each other close in Bar 117, relieved that the ordeal is over. Udolf bravely puts forth a hand, inviting Lorelle to dance once more with him, and the music then recommences in Bar 120 taking the two of them in a steadily more exuberant dance together through to the end of the scene.

♩ = 140
Flute
Oboe
Clarinet in B♭
Bassoon
Horn in F
Trumpet in C
Cornet in B♭
Trombone
Tuba
Timpani
♩ = 140
Cymbals
Violin I
Violin II
Viola
Violoncello
Double Bass

9

Fl.

Ob.

Cl.

Bsn.

Hn.

C Tpt.

Cor.

Tbn.

Tba.

Timp.

Cym.

Vln. I

Vln. II

Vla.

Vc.

Db.

17

Fl.

Ob.

Cl.

Bsn.

Hn.

C Tpt.

Cor.

Tbn.

Tba.

Timp.

Cym.

Vln. I

Vln. II

Vla.

Vc.

Db.

24
Fl.
Ob.
Cl.
Bsn.
Hn.
C Tpt.
Cor.
Tbn.
Tba.
Timp.
Cym.
Vln. I
Vln. II
Vla.
Vc.
Db.

31
Fl.
Ob.
Cl.
Bsn.
Hn.
C Tpt.
Cor.
Tbn.
Tba.
Timp.
Cym.
Vln. I
Vln. II
Vla.
Vc.
Db.

39
Fl.
Ob.
Cl.
Bsn.
Hn.
C Tpt.
Cor.
Tbn.
Tba.
Timp.
Cym.
Vln. I
Vln. II
Vla.
Vc.
Db.

46
Fl.
Ob.
Cl.
Bsn.
Hn.
C Tpt.
Cor.
Tbn.
Tba.
Timp.
Cym.
Vln. I
Vln. II
Vla.
Vc.
Db.

52

Fl.

Ob.

Cl.

Bsn.

Hn.

C Tpt.

Cor.

Tbn.

Tba.

Timp.

Cym.

Vln. I

Vln. II

Vla.

Vc.

Db.

58
Fl.
Ob.
Cl.
Bsn.
Hn.
C Tpt.
Cor.
Tbn.
Tba.
Timp.
Cym.
Vln. I
Vln. II
Vla.
Vc.
Db.

68
Fl.
Ob.
Cl.
Bsn.
Hn.
C Tpt.
Cor.
Tbn.
Tba.
Timp.
Cym.
Vln. I
Vln. II
Vla.
Vc.
Db.

78

Fl.

Ob.

Cl.

Bsn.

Hn.

C Tpt.

Cor.

Tbn.

Tba.

Timp.

Cym.

Vln. I

Vln. II

Vla.

Vc.

Db.

85
Fl.
Ob.
Cl.
Bsn.
Hn.
C Tpt.
Cor.
Tbn.
Tba.
Timp.
Cym.
Vln. I
Vln. II
Vla.
Vc.
Db.

92

Fl.

Ob.

Cl.

Bsn.

Hn.

C Tpt.

Cor.

Tbn.

Tba.

Timp.

Cym.

Vln. I

Vln. II

Vla.

Vc.

Db.

98
Fl.
Ob.
Cl.
Bsn.
Hn.
C Tpt.
Cor.
Tbn.
Tba.
Timp.
Cym.
Vln. I
Vln. II
Vla.
Vc.
Db.

105
Fl.
Ob.
Cl.
Bsn.
Hn.
C Tpt.
Cor.
Tbn.
Tba.
Timp.
Cym.
Vln. I
Vln. II
Vla.
Vc.
Db.

114
Fl.
Ob.
Cl.
Bsn.
Hn.
C Tpt.
Cor.
Tbn.
Tba.
Timp.
Cym.
Vln. I
Vln. II
Vla.
Vc.
Db.

123

Fl.

Ob.

Cl.

Bsn.

Hn.

C Tpt.

Cor.

Tbn.

Tba.

Timp.

Cym.

Vln. I

Vln. II

Vla.

Vc.

Db.

129
Fl.
Ob.
Cl.
Bsn.
Hn.
C Tpt.
Cor.
Tbn.
Tba.
Timp.
Cym.
Vln. I
Vln. II
Vla.
Vc.
Db.

136
Fl.
Ob.
Cl.
Bsn.
Hn.
C Tpt.
Cor.
Tbn.
Tba.
Timp.
Cym.
Vln. I
Vln. II
Vla.
Vc.
Db.

144
rall.
Fl.
Ob.
Cl.
Bsn.
Hn.
C Tpt.
Cor.
Tbn.
Tba.
Timp.
rall.
Cym.
Vln. I
Vln. II
Vla.
Vc.
Db.

150
Fl.
Ob.
Cl.
Bsn.
Hn.
C Tpt.
Cor.
Tbn.
Tba.
Timp.
tr
Cym.
Vln. I
Vln. II
Vla.
Vc.
Db.

156
Fl.
Ob.
Cl.
Bsn.
Hn.
C Tpt.
Cor.
Tbn.
Tba.
Timp.
Cym.
Vln. I
Vln. II
Vla.
Vc.
Db.

ACT II

Scene IV – The Mountain Top

High on a mountain peak Daethon sits in anguish, crying for his lost love as the thunder and lightning surround him. He appears to be alone amongst the craggy outcrops of rock when movements in the darkness suddenly make it clear that the Vampires have come and are around him. He recoils but his grief makes him so weak that he can do nothing. Ambrogio appears in a red glare and comes to him. Daethon falls to his knees, telling Ambrogio all that happened, saying he is innocent of the murder and that he needs Ambrogio's help. Ambrogio had promised him 100 years of joy with the Prince and now Daethon has nothing. Being ancient and wise, the Darklord sees at work in the tale the magic and trickery of the Harpy. Daethon swears revenge but Ambrogio quiets him and tells him to stay in the safety of the Dark Mountain. He tells Daethon however that he shall procure his happiness for him. Daethon remains alone in sadness after Ambrogio leaves, but the Darklord now has a mission ahead of him.

Choreography, Costume and Set Notes

- Daethon is dressed in black with a black cape that billows in the wind; in the opening of the scene real wind blows (wind machine), and flashes of lightning and thunder help to set the stage on the mountain top as initially Daethon sits immobile with his back to the audience in the tempest.

- Daethon slowly rises in Bars 9 and 10 and then starts to dance a slow and mournful solo to express his sadness, misery and anger; the wind dies down to nothing by this point and the lightning and thunder cease, but the light is the light of the stars. The dance needs to be filled with all Daethon's mixed and furious emotions and he can several times fall to the floor and call up to the heavens in anger.

- In Bar 35 the Vampires appear and dance around Daethon before Ambrogio then appears in a flash of dark red light in Bar 43

☙ In Bar 59 Daethon falls to his knees before Ambrogio and tells him the whole tale whilst the Vampires dance; in Bar 67 Ambrogio quiets him and showing his anger explains that he shall make all things right before sweeping off stage to leave Daethon prone in grief.

♩ = 110
Piccolo
Flute
Oboe
Clarinet in B♭
Horn in F
Trumpet in C
Trombone
tr
Timpani
♩ = 110
Cymbals
Violin I
Violin II
Viola
Violoncello
Double Bass

5
Picc.
Fl.
Ob.
Cl.
Hn.
C Tpt.
Tbn.
(tr)
Timp.
Cym.
pizz.
Vln. I
Vln. II
Vla.
Vc.
Db.

10
Picc.
Fl.
Ob.
Cl.
Hn.
C Tpt.
Tbn.
Timp.
Cym.
nat.
Vln. I
Vln. II
Vla.
Vc.
Db.

15
Picc.
Fl.
Ob.
Cl.
Hn.
C Tpt.
Tbn.
Timp.
Cym.
Vln. I
Vln. II
Vla.
Vc.
Db.

19
Picc.
Fl.
Ob.
Cl.
Hn.
C Tpt.
Tbn.
Timp.
Cym.
Vln. I
Vln. II
Vla.
Vc.
Db.

23
Picc.
Fl.
Ob.
Cl.
Hn.
C Tpt.
Tbn.
Timp.
Cym.
Vln. I
Vln. II
Vla.
Vc.
Db.

27
Picc.
Fl.
Ob.
Cl.
Hn.
C Tpt.
Tbn.
Timp.
Cym.
Vln. I
Vln. II
Vla.
Vc.
Db.

31

Picc.

Fl.

Ob.

Cl.

Hn.

C Tpt.

Tbn.

Timp.

Cym.

Vln. I

Vln. II

Vla.

Vc.

Db.

35

Picc.

Fl.

Ob.

Cl.

Hn.

C Tpt.

Tbn.

Timp.

Cym.

Vln. I

Vln. II

Vla.

Vc.

Db.

39
Picc.
Fl.
Ob.
Cl.
Hn.
C Tpt.
Tbn.
Timp.
Cym.
Vln. I
Vln. II
Vla.
Vc.
Db.

43
Picc.
Fl.
Ob.
Cl.
Hn.
C Tpt.
Tbn.
Timp.
Cym.
Vln. I
Vln. II
Vla.
Vc.
Db.

46
Picc.
Fl.
Ob.
Cl.
Hn.
C Tpt.
Tbn.
Timp.
Cym.
Vln. I
Vln. II
Vla.
Vc.
Db.

49
Picc.
Fl.
Ob.
Cl.
Hn.
C Tpt.
Tbn.
Timp.
Cym.
Vln. I
Vln. II
Vla.
Vc.
Db.

52
Picc.
Fl.
Ob.
Cl.
Hn.
C Tpt.
Tbn.
Timp.
Cym.
Vln. I
Vln. II
Vla.
Vc.
Db.

55
Picc.
Fl.
Ob.
Cl.
Hn.
C Tpt.
Tbn.
Timp.
Cym.
Vln. I
Vln. II
Vla.
Vc.
Db.

58
Picc.
Fl.
Ob.
Cl.
Hn.
C Tpt.
Tbn.
Timp.
Cym.
Vln. I
Vln. II
Vla.
Vc.
Db.

62
Picc.
Fl.
Ob.
Cl.
Hn.
C Tpt.
Tbn.
Timp.
Cym.
Vln. I
Vln. II
Vla.
Vc.
Db.

66
Picc.
Fl.
Ob.
Cl.
Hn.
C Tpt.
Tbn.
Timp.
Cym.
Vln. I
Vln. II
Vla.
Vc.
Db.

70
Picc.
Fl.
Ob.
Cl.
Hn.
C Tpt.
Tbn.
Timp.
Cym.
Vln. I
Vln. II
Vla.
Vc.
Db.

73
rall.
Picc.
Fl.
Ob.
Cl.
Hn.
C Tpt.
Tbn.
Timp.
rall.
Cym.
Vln. I
Vln. II
Vla.
Vc.
Db.

ACT II

Scene V – Lorelle's Compulsion

Lorelle walks on stage, pregnant now with the new heir, and she stands at her window contemplating her kingdom. Suddenly in the rear of the bedchamber a dark shadow appears. It is Ambrogio and he slowly dances about her as she falls under his spell. He compels her to stand in the centre of the room and they dance together as he weaves a compulsion in her mind. He creates an image of her child lying in the crib and compels her to take a dagger and stab the child to death. The illusion breaks but as Ambrogio fades into the blackness of the night Lorelle is left holding the dagger and abruptly making the stabbing motions as the compulsion to kill her own child remains within her. She drops the dagger in horror at what she must do, but then as if in a trance picks the dagger up again and again, making the same stabbing motion, unable to stop herself. The scene closes with her lain on the floor in horror, the dagger still in her hand, to the dark laughter of the Darklord echoing around her.

Choreography, Costume and Set Notes

- The Darklord is dressed in his red and black and Lorelle in the garments of the bedchamber; the Darklord appears in Bar 17 initially only as a dark figure but then as he moves forward he is lit and Lorelle is brought under his spell

- As the two of them start to dance a pas de deux, the Darklord holds out his hand at her eyes and she dances as if entranced.

- From Bar 49 the dance together becomes more frantic and Ambrogio subjects Lorelle to so many spins and turns that she is quite dizzy and off balance before suddenly pulling a dagger from his robes in Bar 65 and holding it aloft. Lorelle stops dancing and looks in horror at the dagger but she cannot move.

- Ambrogio places the dagger in her hand and makes her dance with it; it is only in Bar 81 that things change, and he brings her to a great mirror on the wall in which suddenly appears an image of herself standing with the dagger held over her baby in her arms (portrayed by another ballerina behind the mirror wearing identical attire). Lorelle watches in horror with her hands over her mouth as the ballerina in the mirror turns away but then clearly stabs the child with the dagger, the child now being obscured.

- The mirror returns to normal and from Bar 97 Lorelle staggers back in horror and drops the dagger to the floor, then falls back to the floor herself not believing the evil that is before her; Ambrogio moves menacingly towards her. However then in Bar 113 he makes a grasping motion with his hand and Lorelle is again compelled to her feet and with the compulsion he yet again forces her to pick up the dagger.

- From Bar 129 to the end of the scene Lorelle is made to dance with the dagger, and although she tries to drop it she is always forced to pick it up again. Ambrogio recedes from the scene before the music finishes but Lorelle is left whirling around with the dagger in her hand and as the scene ends she falls to the floor with the dagger still in hand.

- Lighting can be used to great effect, so deep red light for moments of compulsion for example and moonlight for the rest of the scene.

♩ = 135
Flute
Clarinet in B♭
Bassoon
Horn in F
Trumpet in C
Trombone
Tuba
Timpani
Cymbals
Choir
♩ = 135
Violin I
Violin II
ppp
Viola
Violoncello
Double Bass

14
Fl.
Cl.
Bsn.
Hn.
C Tpt.
Tbn.
Tba.
Timp.
Cym.
Choir
Vln. I
Vln. II
Vla.
Vc.
Db.

24

Fl.

Cl.

Bsn.

Hn.

C Tpt.

Tbn.

Tba.

Timp.

Cym.

Choir

pp

Vln. I

Vln. II

mf

Vla.

Vc.

Db.

33
Fl.
Cl.
Bsn.
Hn.
C Tpt.
Tbn.
Tba.
Timp.
Cym.
Choir
Vln. I
Vln. II
Vla.
Vc.
Db.

42

Fl.

Cl.

Bsn.

Hn.

C Tpt.

Tbn.

Tba.

Timp.

Cym.

mf

Choir

mf

Vln. I

Vln. II

Vla.

Vc.

Db.

51
Fl.
Cl.
Bsn.
Hn.
C Tpt.
Tbn.
Tba.
Timp.
Cym.
Choir
Vln. I
Vln. II
Vla.
Vc.
Db.

60
Fl.
Cl.
Bsn.
Hn.
C Tpt.
Tbn.
Tba.
Timp.
Cym.
Choir
Vln. I
Vln. II
Vla.
Vc.
Db.

69
Fl.
Cl.
Bsn.
Hn.
C Tpt.
Tbn.
Tba.
Timp.
Cym.
Choir
Vln. I
Vln. II
Vla.
Vc.
Db.

79
Fl.
Cl.
Bsn.
Hn.
C Tpt.
Tbn.
Tba.
Timp.
tr
Cym.
Choir
Vln. I
Vln. II
Vla.
Vc.
Db.

88
Fl.
Cl.
Bsn.
Hn.
C Tpt.
mp
Tbn.
Tba.
Timp.
Cym.
Choir
mp
Vln. I
Vln. II
Vla.
Vc.
Db.

97
Fl.
Cl.
Bsn.
Hn.
C Tpt.
Tbn.
Tba.
Timp.
Cym.
mf
Choir
mf
Vln. I
Vln. II
Vla.
Vc.
Db.

106
Fl.
Cl.
Bsn.
Hn.
C Tpt.
Tbn.
Tba.
Timp.
Cym.
Choir
Vln. I
Vln. II
Vla.
Vc.
Db.

115

Fl.

Cl.

Bsn.

Hn.

C Tpt.

Tbn.

Tba.

Timp.

Cym.

Choir

Vln. I

Vln. II

Vla.

Vc.

Db.

124
Fl.
Cl.
Bsn.
Hn.
C Tpt.
Tbn.
Tba.
Timp.
tr
tr
Cym.
Choir
Vln. I
Vln. II
Vla.
Vc.
Db.

133
molto rall.
Fl.
Cl.
Bsn.
Hn.
C Tpt.
Tbn.
Tba.
Timp.
Cym.
Choir
molto rall.
Vln. I
Vln. II
Vla.
Vc.
Db.

139
Fl.
Cl.
Bsn.
Hn.
C Tpt.
Tbn.
Tba.
tr
Timp.
Cym.
Choir
Vln. I
Vln. II
Vla.
Vc.
Db.

ACT III

ENTR'ACTE

ACT III

Scene I – A Royal Baby

Princess Lorelle is in her chambers having just given birth to her child, and outside the Nobles and Prince Udolf dance with excitement and apprehension whilst the Ladies-in-Waiting dressed as nurses inside fuss around the Princess. One of the Ladies brings the new-born child to be shown to the Prince. The child is greeted with great joy and whilst the Princess rests, the Prince shows the child to King Haelan who is overjoyed. After great excitement and dancing to celebrate the arrival of the new-born, the child is left with his mother into the gathering evening, for she is now tired, and the Ladies shoo away all the men to give Lorelle some peace. Left alone with her new child in her chambers the Princess feels a gathering darkness in the gloom outside and red begins to stain the sky. In fear she holds her baby to her. Then of a sudden she finds herself rising from her bed, leaving the child lying there. With Ambrogio's terrifying visage haunting her she goes to her dressing table and pulls a dagger from the drawer. Despite all her efforts to stop herself she draws nearer to the bed and as the thunderous darkness beats against her she at last is made to drive the dagger into her newly born child's heart, collapsing in floods of tears the moment she has done so. The laughs of Ambrogio she can hear in her ears, and she mourns the loss of her child; Udolf enters and is stunned, horrified and grief-stricken. They mourn together but Udolf cannot look at Lorelle after what she did. Then suddenly in a flash of magic Gullveig appears, come for her prize, the unspoiled heart of Lorelle's firstborn child. The Harpy's fury is terrible at what Lorelle has done and with her magic she raises a thunderous storm and calls forth the ghostly blue and white Spirits who dance around and torment the pair whilst Gullveig, raised to her full height brings pain to them both with every step they take. The Harpy brings Lorelle to her knees to watch and then raises up Udolf and strikes him down dead as punishment for what Lorelle has done. The Spirits laugh and Gullveig leaves as Lorelle lies weeping and crying for her lost child and her lost consort.

Choreography, Costume and Set Notes

- The scene opens with the stage split, so on stage left the Nobles and the Prince dance together in apprehension whilst behind a partition on stage right Lorelle lies in bed with her child and the Ladies fuss about her.

- One of the Ladies brings the child out to the Prince in Bar 59 whilst the Nobles continue to dance, and the Prince shows the child to King Haelan who enters and then leaves again from stage left.

- In Bar 91 the dancing finally ceases as all the Ladies come out to shoo away the men. One lady takes the child from the Prince and takes him back to his mother in bed. All then leave, and the light softens around the bed to appear like moonlight so that all that can be seen is the mother with her child in the bed.

- From Bar 107 Lorelle comforts the child in the bed then suddenly in Bar 119 she places the child aside on the bed and in a trance rises from the bed and goes to the chest of drawers. As Bar 123 starts she raises a dagger from the drawer and slowly holds it aloft as the light starts to go red and the visage of Ambrogio appears faintly in the mirror on the wall (this can be projected).

- From Bar 139 Lorelle starts to try to fight the compulsion but the red light grows stronger and she is brought slowly over the bed before she finally plunges the dagger into her own child at Bar 157.

- Lorelle then falls to her knees and the light returns to the normal light of moonlight coming in through the window. Right up to Bar 194 she dances a slow dance of mourning, after initially weeping on her knees for a time. In Bar 179 Udolf enters and falls to his own knees in horror seeing what has happened; Lorelle pleads with him for forgiveness and they dance a pas de deux filled with grief and anger where neither can face each other.

- In Bar 195 Gullveig suddenly appears and the Spirits then arrive and dance around the tortured pair held in the Harpy's furious magic; thunder and lightning can be used here to great effect.

- In Bar 247 Gullveig lifts up Udolf using her magic and this can be done with some cunning use of wires under Udolf's arms, so he is actually lifted off the floor as Gullveig holds out her hand as though holding his throat with magic; then in Bar 251 she snaps his neck with her magic and drops his body to the floor in a heap before marching off stage as the Spirits dance off. Lorelle cries out at Udolf's death and, still pinned to the ground by magic, reaches out her hands in grief and horror at her dead love as the scene ends and the lights go down. When in the ballet real screams are needed it is important that real screams are made to accentuate the horror.

♩ = 120
Piccolo
Flute
Oboe
Clarinet in B♭
Horn in F
Trumpet in C
Trumpet in B♭
Tuba
Timpani
tr
♩ = 120
Cymbals
Tubular Bells
Violin I
Violin II
Viola
Violoncello
Double Bass

11
Picc.
Fl.
Ob.
Cl.
Hn.
C Tpt.
Tpt.
Tba.
Timp.
Cym.
Tub. B.
Vln. I
Vln. II
Vla.
Vc.
Db.

22
Picc.
Fl.
Ob.
Cl.
Hn.
C Tpt.
Tpt.
Tba.
Timp.
Cym.
Tub. B.
Vln. I
Vln. II
pizz.
nat.
Vla.
p
Vc.
pizz.
Db.
p

33
Picc.
Fl.
Ob.
Cl.
Hn.
C Tpt.
Tpt.
Tba.
Timp.
Cym.
Tub. B.
Vln. I
Vln. II
Vla.
nat.
Vc.
Db.

43
Picc.
Fl.
Ob.
Cl.
Hn.
C Tpt.
Tpt.
Tba.
Timp.
Cym.
Tub. B.
Vln. I
Vln. II
Vla.
Vc.
Db.

54
Picc.
Fl.
Ob.
Cl.
Hn.
C Tpt.
Tpt.
Tba.
Timp.
Cym.
Tub. B.
Vln. I
Vln. II
Vla.
Vc.
Db.

64
Picc.
Fl.
Ob.
Cl.
Hn.
C Tpt.
Tpt.
Tba.
Timp.
Cym.
Tub. B.
Vln. I
Vln. II
Vla.
Vc.
Db.

74

Picc.

Fl.

Ob.

Cl.

Hn.

C Tpt.

Tpt.

Tba.

Timp.

Cym.

Tub. B.

Vln. I

Vln. II

Vla.

Vc.

Db.

84
Picc.
Fl.
Ob.
Cl.
Hn.
C Tpt.
Tpt.
Tba.
Timp.
Cym.
Tub. B.
Vln. I
Vln. II
Vla.
Vc.
Db.
mp

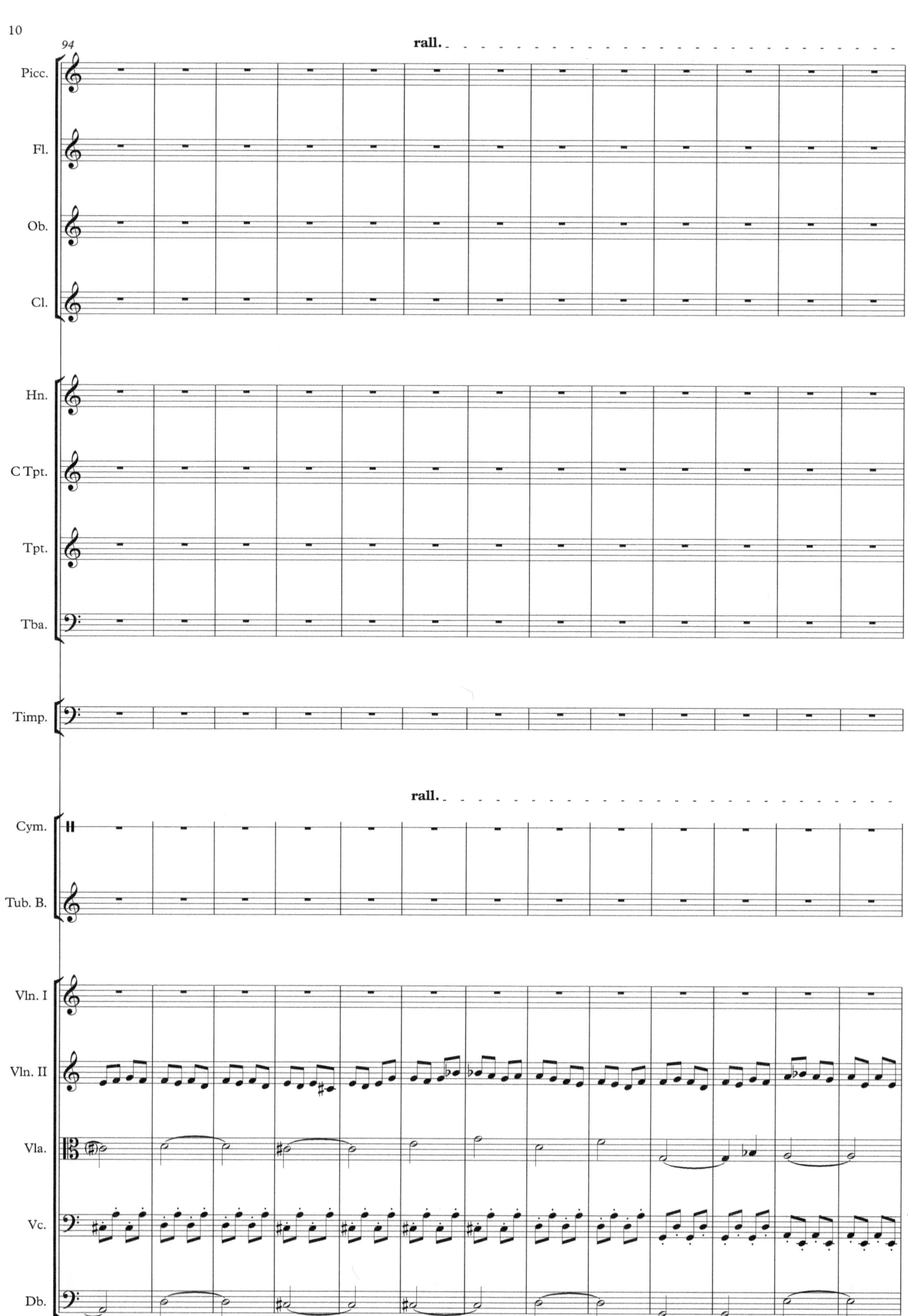
94
rall.
Picc.
Fl.
Ob.
Cl.
Hn.
C Tpt.
Tpt.
Tba.
Timp.
rall.
Cym.
Tub. B.
Vln. I
Vln. II
Vla.
Vc.
Db.

107
Picc.
Fl.
mp
Ob.
mp
Cl.
Hn.
C Tpt.
Tpt.
Tba.
Timp.
Cym.
Tub. B.
Vln. I
p
Vln. II
Vla.
Vc.
Db.

115
Picc.
Fl.
Ob.
Cl.
Hn.
C Tpt.
Tpt.
Tba.
Timp.
Cym.
Tub. B.
Vln. I
Vln. II
Vla.
Vc.
Db.

123
Picc.
Fl.
Ob.
Cl.
Hn.
C Tpt.
Tpt.
Tba.
Timp.
Cym.
Tub. B.
Vln. I
Vln. II
Vla.
Vc.
Db.
mf

131
Picc.
Fl.
Ob.
Cl.
Hn.
C Tpt.
Tpt.
Tba.
Timp.
Cym.
Tub. B.
Vln. I
Vln. II
Vla.
Vc.
Db.

139
Picc.
Fl.
Ob.
Cl.
Hn.
C Tpt.
Tpt.
Tba.
Timp.
Cym.
Tub. B.
Vln. I
Vln. II
Vla.
Vc.
Db.

146
Picc.
Fl.
Ob.
Cl.
Hn.
C Tpt.
Tpt.
Tba.
Timp.
Cym.
Tub. B.
Vln. I
Vln. II
Vla.
Vc.
Db.

153

molto rall.

Picc.
Fl.
Ob.
Cl.
Hn.
C Tpt.
Tpt.
Tba.
Timp.

mp

tr

molto rall.

Cym.
Tub. B.
Vln. I
Vln. II
Vla.
Vc.
Db.

pp

pp

165
Picc.
Fl.
Ob.
Cl.
Hn.
C Tpt.
Tpt.
Tba.
Timp.
Cym.
Tub. B.
Vln. I
Vln. II
pp
Vla.
Vc.
Db.

179
Picc.
mp
Fl.
Ob.
Cl.
Hn.
C Tpt.
Tpt.
Tba.
Timp.
Cym.
Tub. B.
Vln. I
pp
Vln. II
Vla.
Vc.
Db.
pp

187
Picc.
Fl.
Ob.
Cl.
Hn.
C Tpt.
Tpt.
Tba.
Timp.
Cym.
Tub. B.
Vln. I
Vln. II
Vla.
Vc.
Db.

♩ = 90
195
Picc.
Fl.
Ob.
Cl.
Hn.
mf
C Tpt.
Tpt.
Tba.
mf
Timp.
mf
♩ = 90
Cym.
Tub. B.
Vln. I
mf
Vln. II
mf
Vla.
mf
pizz.
Vc.
mf
Db.
mf

203
Picc.
Fl.
Ob.
Cl.
Hn.
C Tpt.
Tpt.
Tba.
Timp.
Cym.
Tub. B.
Vln. I
Vln. II
Vla.
Vc.
Db.

211
Picc.
Fl.
Ob.
Cl.
Hn.
C Tpt.
Tpt.
Tba.
Timp.
Cym.
Tub. B.
Vln. I
Vln. II
Vla.
nat.
Vc.
Db.

219

Picc.

Fl.

Ob.

Cl.

Hn.

C Tpt.

Tpt.

Tba.

Timp.

Cym.

Tub. B.

Vln. I

Vln. II

Vla.

Vc.

Db.

227
Picc.
Fl.
Ob.
Cl.
Hn.
C Tpt.
Tpt.
Tba.
Timp.
Cym.
Tub. B.
Vln. I
Vln. II
Vla.
Vc.
Db.

235

Picc.
Fl.
Ob.
Cl.
Hn.
C Tpt.
Tpt.
Tba.
Timp.
Cym.
Tub. B.
Vln. I
Vln. II
Vla.
Vc.
Db.

243
Picc.
Fl.
Ob.
Cl.
Hn.
C Tpt.
Tpt.
Tba.
Timp.
tr
Cym.
Tub. B.
Vln. I
Vln. II
Vla.
Vc.
Db.

ACT III

Scene II – A Deal with the Harpy

The Harpy has returned to her realm and there the Spirits try to comfort her with their entertaining dances, but she is inconsolable at her loss of the heart she had been promised. Suddenly Daethon enters the ghostly chamber and kneels before the Harpy, bowing low. She walks to him and speaks with him, for she knows nothing of Ambrogio's cunning and sees only Daethon's loss and is saddened by it. Daethon beseeches the Harpy to return his lost love, Arundel, from beyond the grave and in return he will procure a heart for her with the powers of a Vampire held within it. The Harpy agrees and gives to Daethon a pendant that will allow him to seduce the Princess and the ring to show Haelan to reveal Lorelle and Udolf's treachery. Daethon leaves and the Harpy dances solemnly and reverently with the Spirits, with anticipation of the new heart that they shall soon receive.

Choreography, Costume and Set Notes

- Lights come up on Bar 5; the Spirits don't dare enter stage until Bar 19 to comfort Gullveig and before then she wanders and sits and wanders and sits, etc., with her anger and sadness evident as she prowls her demesne. The choreography for this piece can be very freely down to the choreographer to bring out the nature of the Spirits and the fury of Gullveig; the costuming needs to be that of the faerie realm, as does the set design. Dancing en pointe needs to be a centrepiece quality of this entire scene since the Spirits have great power; the corps of Spirits, all female must astound the audience with the synchrony and beauty.

- Daethon enters and makes his impassioned plea in Bar 59 before dancing with Gullveig and the Spirits; whilst he makes his plea and Gullveig listens the Spirits still dance around vigorously. Gullveig gives him the pendant and the ring in Bars 83 and 87 respectively and he then leaves with gratitude in Bar 90, running from stage, leaving Gullveig and the Spirits to dance solemnly to the end of the scene but with great joy and reverence at what is to come.

♩ = 100
Piccolo
Flute
Oboe
Clarinet in B♭
Bassoon
Horn in F
Timpani
Cymbals
Choir
Celesta
♩ = 100
Violin I
tremolo
ppp
Violin II
tremolo
ppp
Viola
tremolo
ppp
Violoncello
tremolo
ppp
Double Bass
tremolo
ppp

15
Picc.
Fl.
mp
Ob.
p
Cl.
Bsn.
Hn.
Timp.
Cym.
Choir
Cel.
nat.
Vln. I
Vln. II
nat.
Vla.
mp
nat.
Vc.
p
nat.
Db.
p

23
Picc.
Fl.
Ob.
Cl.
Bsn.
Hn.
Timp.
Cym.
Choir
Cel.
Vln. I
Vln. II
Vla.
Vc.
Db.
mp
p
pp
nat.

30
Picc.
Fl.
Ob.
Cl.
Bsn.
Hn.
Timp.
Cym.
Choir
Cel.
Vln. I
Vln. II
Vla.
Vc.
Db.
mf
mf
mf
p

36
Picc.
Fl.
Ob.
Cl.
Bsn.
Hn.
Timp.
Cym.
Choir
Cel.
Vln. I
Vln. II
Vla.
Vc.
Db.

42
Picc.
Fl.
mf
Ob.
Cl.
p
Bsn.
mp
Hn.
p
Timp.
Cym.
Choir
Cel.
mp
Vln. I
Vln. II
Vla.
Vc.
Db.

48

Picc.

Fl.

Ob.

Cl.

Bsn.

Hn.

Timp.

Cym.

Choir

Cel.

Vln. I

Vln. II

Vla.

Vc.

Db.

mf *mf* *mf* *mp* *mf* *mf* *mf*

55
Picc.
Fl.
Ob.
Cl.
Bsn.
Hn.
Timp.
Cym.
Choir
Cel.
Vln. I
Vln. II
Vla.
Vc.
Db.
mf
tr
f
p
tremolo
nat.

62
Picc.
Fl.
Ob.
Cl.
Bsn.
Hn.
Timp.
Cym.
Choir
Cel.
Vln. I
Vln. II
Vla.
Vc.
Db.
p
mf

69
Picc.
Fl.
Ob.
Cl.
Bsn.
Hn.
Timp.
Cym.
Choir
Cel.
Vln. I
Vln. II
Vla.
Vc.
Db.

76
Picc.
Fl.
Ob.
Cl.
Bsn.
Hn.
Timp.
Cym.
Choir
Cel.
Vln. I
Vln. II
Vla.
Vc.
Db.

83
Picc.
Fl.
Ob.
Cl.
Bsn.
Hn.
Timp.
tr
Cym.
f
Choir
Cel.
Vln. I
Vln. II
Vla.
Vc.
Db.

90
Picc.
Fl.
p
Ob.
Cl.
Bsn.
Hn.
(tr)
Timp.
Cym.
Choir
ppp
Cel.
Vln. I
Vln. II
Vla.
ppp
Vc.
ppp
Db.
ppp

97
Picc.
Fl.
Ob.
p
pp
Cl.
Bsn.
Hn.
Timp.
Cym.
Choir
ppp
Cel.
Vln. I
Vln. II
Vla.
Vc.
Db.

ACT III

Scene III – Daethon & Lorelle

Wearing the Harpy's pendant, Daethon enters the King's Palace with none of the nobles recognising him; he professes to be the Prince of Bourgogne when questioned by the King as to his identity whilst the Nobles dance. A festival is being held for the King's return from battle in the East, but the Princess sits alone and unloved at the table, filled with sadness and inconsolable, both by the courtiers who seek to dance with her and by the King who tries to comfort her. Daethon however dances with the Nobles and then approaches her and brings her into his will, seducing her and in the end dancing with her. They dance together, and the onlooking court is amazed with Daethon's dancing. The King is pleased that a new Prince has caught his daughter's eye and he watches pleased whilst they dance, with the scene ending with Lorelle in Daethon's hold.

Choreography, Costume and Set Notes

- As the scene opens the King comes on stage with all the Nobles and Ladies in attendance and the setting is again the Great Hall set for a feast. Some of the Nobles are dressed in military attire and behave as guards to the King. Lorelle follows disconsolately and collapses herself onto a seat in one of the corners not wishing to be involved.

- The whole company dances and then come Bar 31 the dance quiets and the King approaches his daughter to try to comfort her and get her to come into the festivities, but she refuses. In Bar 35 Daethon enters from the opposite side of the stage or from the rear of the stage depending on choreography, dressed in a deep royal purple as the Prince of Bourgogne, and catches the King's eye. The King approaches and speaks with him, Daethon of course bowing low, and the King then invites him to join the dancing. The original theme recommences in Bar 47 and Daethon joins the dance centre stage, showing off and impressing all with his dancing.

☙ In Bar 65 Daethon breaks away from the dancing and approaches Lorelle, who has been watching him with interest. He slowly coaxes her to stand and with a bow he ingratiates himself. He moves her towards the centre stage and helps her become part of the dancing, slowly initially but then with joyful exuberance they lead the dance from Bar 81. The dance continues with more and more pomp involving the whole company in some spectacular choreography up to a dramatic ending in Bar 96, at which point the whole company remains motionless in their final poses for applause.

☙ The Nobles and Ladies then recede to take their places at the large U-shaped table but Daethon and Lorelle remain centre stage and from Bar 100 they commence a pas de deux with occasional accentuation by lighting, placing them in a spotlight as they dance together before the entire court. Their dance ends both triumphantly and romantically at the end of the scene with the King smiling widely on his throne.

♩ = 120
Piccolo
Flute
Clarinet in B♭
Bassoon
Horn in F
Trumpet in C
Trombone
Tuba
Timpani
♩ = 120
Cymbals
Snare Drum
Violin I
Violin II
Viola
Violoncello
Double Bass
mp
mf

6
Picc.
Fl.
Cl.
Bsn.
Hn.
mf
C Tpt.
mf
Tbn.
mf
Tba.
mf
Timp.
Cym.
S. D.
Vln. I
Vln. II
Vla.
Vc.
Db.

11
Picc.
Fl.
Cl.
Bsn.
Hn.
C Tpt.
Tbn.
Tba.
Timp.
Cym.
S. D.
Vln. I
Vln. II
Vla.
Vc.
Db.
mp

16
Picc.
Fl.
Cl.
mp
Bsn.
mp
Hn.
C Tpt.
mp
Tbn.
mp
Tba.
Timp.
Cym.
S. D.
Vln. I
Vln. II
Vla.
Vc.
Db.

22
Picc.
Fl.
Cl.
Bsn.
Hn.
C Tpt.
Tbn.
Tba.
Timp.
Cym.
S. D.
Vln. I
Vln. II
Vla.
Vc.
Db.
mf

27
Picc.
Fl.
Cl.
Bsn.
Hn.
C Tpt.
Tbn.
Tba.
Timp.
Cym.
S. D.
Vln. I
Vln. II
Vla.
Vc.
Db.
p
mp
p
p
p
p

32

Picc. *mp*

Fl. *mp*

Cl. *mp*

Bsn. *mp*

Hn.

C Tpt.

Tbn.

Tba.

Timp.

Cym.

S. D.

Vln. I *mf*

Vln. II *mp*

Vla. *mp*

Vc. *mp*

Db. *mp*

39
Picc.
Fl.
Cl.
Bsn.
Hn.
C Tpt.
Tbn.
Tba.
Timp.
Cym.
S. D.
Vln. I
Vln. II
Vla.
Vc.
Db.

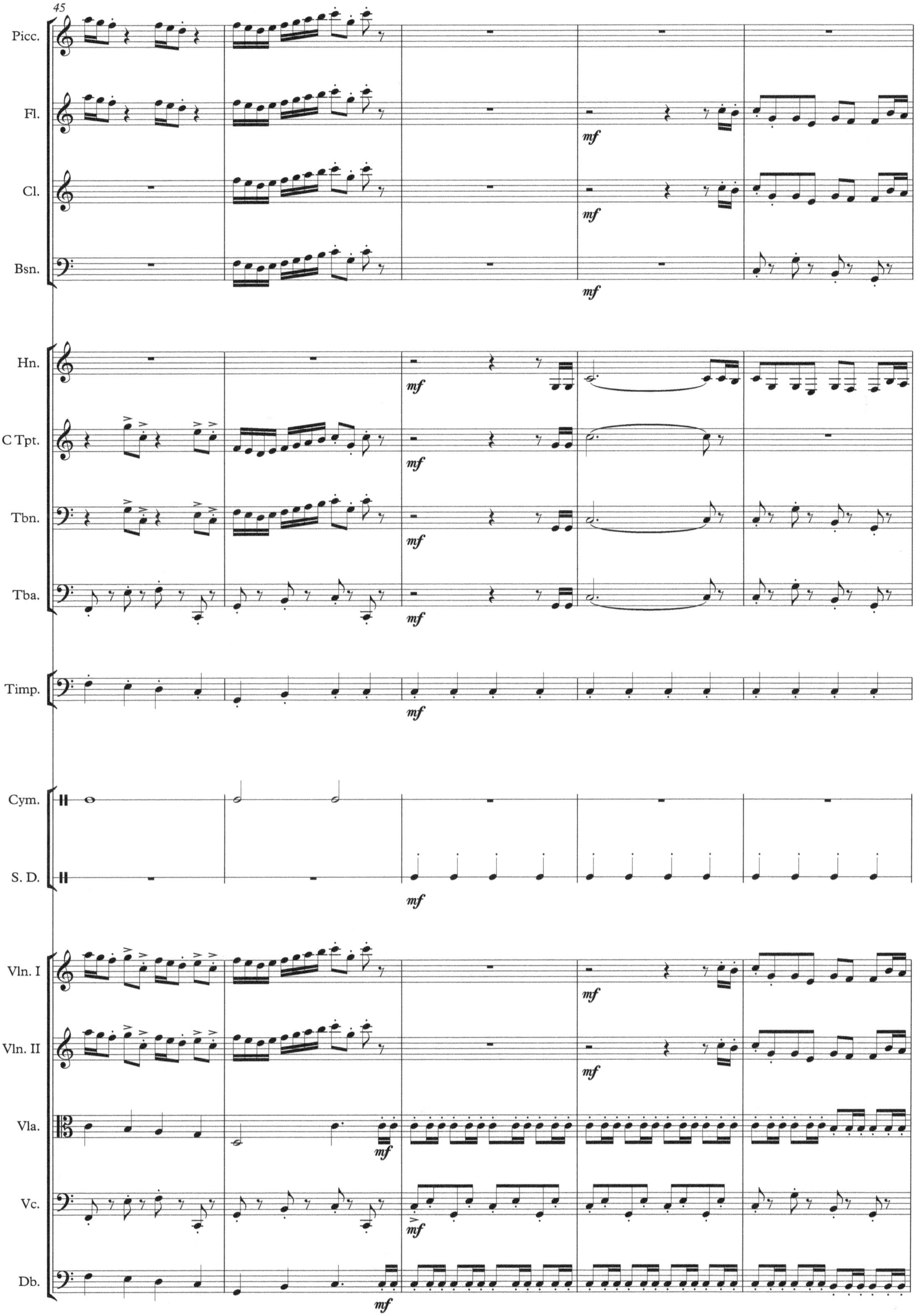

45

Picc.

Fl.

Cl.

Bsn.

Hn.

C Tpt.

Tbn.

Tba.

Timp.

Cym.

S. D.

Vln. I

Vln. II

Vla.

Vc.

Db.

50
Picc.
Fl.
Cl.
Bsn.
Hn.
C Tpt.
Tbn.
Tba.
Timp.
Cym.
S. D.
Vln. I
Vln. II
Vla.
Vc.
Db.
mf

55
Picc.
Fl.
Cl.
Bsn.
Hn.
C Tpt.
Tbn.
Tba.
Timp.
Cym.
S. D.
Vln. I
Vln. II
Vla.
Vc.
Db.

60
Picc.
Fl.
Cl.
Bsn.
Hn.
C Tpt.
Tbn.
Tba.
Timp.
Cym.
S. D.
Vln. I
Vln. II
Vla.
Vc.
Db.

65
Picc.
Fl.
Cl.
Bsn.
Hn.
C Tpt.
Tbn.
Tba.
Timp.
Cym.
S. D.
Vln. I
Vln. II
Vla.
Vc.
Db.
mp
p

71
Picc.
Fl.
mp
Cl.
mp
Bsn.
mp
Hn.
mp
C Tpt.
Tbn.
Tba.
Timp.
Cym.
S. D.
ppp
Vln. I
mp
Vln. II
mp
Vla.
mp
Vc.
mp
Db.
mp

77
Picc.
Fl.
Cl.
Bsn.
Hn.
C Tpt.
Tbn.
Tba.
Timp.
Cym.
S. D.
Vln. I
Vln. II
Vla.
Vc.
Db.
mf
mp
tr

82

Picc.

Fl.

Cl.

Bsn.

Hn.

C Tpt.

Tbn.

Tba.

Timp.

Cym.

S. D.

Vln. I

Vln. II

Vla.

Vc.

Db.

87
Picc.
Fl.
Cl.
Bsn.
Hn.
C Tpt.
Tbn.
Tba.
Timp.
Cym.
S. D.
Vln. I
Vln. II
Vla.
Vc.
Db.
f

92
Picc.
Fl.
Cl.
Bsn.
Hn.
C Tpt.
Tbn.
Tba.
Timp.
Cym.
S. D.
Vln. I
Vln. II
Vla.
Vc.
Db.

98
♩ = 65
Picc.
mp
Fl.
Cl.
Bsn.
Hn.
C Tpt.
Tbn.
Tba.
Timp.
♩ = 65
Cym.
S. D.
Vln. I
Vln. II
Vla.
pp
Vc.
pp
Db.
pp

104
Picc.
Fl.
mp
Cl.
mp
Bsn.
Hn.
C Tpt.
Tbn.
Tba.
Timp.
Cym.
S. D.
Vln. I
Vln. II
pp
Vla.
Vc.
Db.

109
Picc.
Fl.
Cl.
Bsn.
Hn.
C Tpt.
Tbn.
Tba.
Timp.
Cym.
S. D.
Vln. I
mp
Vln. II
Vla.
Vc.
Db.

114
Picc.
Fl.
Cl.
Bsn.
Hn.
C Tpt.
Tbn.
Tba.
Timp.
Cym.
S. D.
Vln. I
Vln. II
Vla.
Vc.
Db.

120

Picc.
mp

Fl.
mp

Cl.
mp

Bsn.
mp

Hn.
mp

C Tpt.
mp

Tbn.
mp

Tba.
mp

Timp.
mp

Cym.

S. D.

Vln. I
mp

Vln. II
mp

Vla.
mp

Vc.
mp

Db.
mp

127
Picc.
Fl.
Cl.
Bsn.
Hn.
C Tpt.
Tbn.
Tba.
Timp.
Cym.
S. D.
Vln. I
Vln. II
Vla.
Vc.
Db.

133

Picc.
Fl.
Cl.
Bsn.
Hn.
C Tpt.
Tbn.
Tba.
Timp.
Cym.
S. D.
Vln. I
Vln. II
Vla.
Vc.
Db.

tr
mf
f

138
Picc.
Fl.
Cl.
Bsn.
Hn.
C Tpt.
Tbn.
Tba.
Timp.
tr
Cym.
S. D.
Vln. I
Vln. II
Vla.
Vc.
Db.
f

143
molto rall.
Picc.
Fl.
Cl.
Bsn.
Hn.
C Tpt.
Tbn.
Tba.
Timp.
molto rall.
Cym.
S. D.
Vln. I
Vln. II
Vla.
Vc.
Db.

147
Picc.
Fl.
Cl.
Bsn.
Hn.
C Tpt.
Tbn.
Tba.
Timp.
Cym.
S. D.
Vln. I
Vln. II
Vla.
Vc.
Db.

ACT III

Scene IV – A Marriage of Convenience

In the King's great cathedral, Daethon solemnly enters with Lorelle and they are wed with the King and all the nobles and ladies in attendance and, after dancing to celebrate, they retire to the bedchamber where Daethon woos her into bed. Then, in a magical storm, Daethon conceives a new child in Lorelle's womb. Daethon's prowess leaves Lorelle tired but filled with joy, yet unbeknownst to them both as they have sex together under the covers, the Spirits of Gullveig appear and dance about the bed, weaving magic and feeling the new soul growing within Lorelle that will soon be theirs.

Choreography, Costume and Set Notes

- The scene opens in a solemn ceremony in the cathedral as Daethon, still in his deep purple as the Prince of Bourgogne, is wedded to Lorelle with the court and the king looking on. One of the dancers who would play another role can act as the priest for the ceremony.

- The ceremony is complete by Bar 9 and the two of them walk out of the cathedral as the choir sings, leaving stage right with all following in a line and then re-entering the stage from backstage in the upstage centre position, as if entering now a new room in the palace. The Servants enter from both stage left and stage right to give drinks to the waiting Nobles and Ladies and the King takes his seat on another throne in one of the corners. Daethon and Lorelle move to centre stage and dance a slow adagio together as their first dance as a married couple.

- From Bar 51 the other Nobles and Ladies join the dance, before all steadily bowing after the dance and taking their leave of the hall between Bars 67 and 84. These bars of music are for a quick set change to the bedroom as Lorelle and Daethon hold each other centre stage, looking at the audience. A spotlight can fall upon them if it makes the scene change less obvious and then the lights rise to reveal them alone in the bedchamber by Bar 85.

❧ From Bar 85 to Bar 100 Daethon seduces Lorelle through his dance and they undress, before in Bar 100 getting under the covers completely obscured from sight but moving as if having sex. From Bar 101 to the end of the scene the lights dim to that of moonlight, with a pale blue light around the bed and the Spirits come from both stage left and stage right, en pointe, and dance around the bed weaving magic with their arms. At Bar 130 Lorelle's hand can suddenly shoot outstretched from under the covers as if climaxing and the whole bed shudder in a hidden climax before the arm and whole bed relaxes just before the lights go down. The idea is to convey the moment of conception without ever actually seeing it.

♩ = 90
Flute
Clarinet in B♭
Bassoon
Horn in F
Trumpet in C
Trombone
Tuba
Timpani
Cymbals
♩ = 90
Choir
mf
Violin I
Violin II
Viola
Violoncello
Double Bass

11
Fl.
Cl.
Bsn.
f
Hn.
mf
C Tpt.
Tbn.
Tba.
Timp.
Cym.
p
Choir
p
Vln. I
Vln. II
Vla.
Vc.
Db.

21

Fl.

Cl.

Bsn.

mf

Hn.

C Tpt.

Tbn.

Tba.

Timp.

Cym.

Choir

Vln. I

Vln. II

Vla.

Vc.

Db.

30
Fl.
Cl.
Bsn.
Hn.
C Tpt.
Tbn.
mf
Tba.
Timp.
Cym.
mp
Choir
mp
Vln. I
mf
Vln. II
Vla.
Vc.
Db.

39
Fl.
Cl.
Bsn.
Hn.
C Tpt.
Tbn.
Tba.
Timp.
Cym.
Choir
Vln. I
Vln. II
Vla.
Vc.
Db.

47
Fl.
Cl.
Bsn.
Hn.
C Tpt.
Tbn.
Tba.
Timp.
Cym.
Choir
Vln. I
Vln. II
Vla.
Vc.
Db.

55
molto rall.
Fl.
Cl.
Bsn.
Hn.
C Tpt.
Tbn.
Tba.
Timp.
Cym.
molto rall.
Choir
Vln. I
Vln. II
Vla.
Vc.
Db.

63
♩ = 120
Fl.
Cl.
Bsn.
Hn.
C Tpt.
Tbn.
Tba.
Timp.
Cym.
Choir
Vln. I
Vln. II
Vla.
Vc.
Db.
mf

72
Fl.
Cl.
Bsn.
Hn.
C Tpt.
Tbn.
Tba.
Timp.
Cym.
Choir
Vln. I
Vln. II
Vla.
Vc.
Db.

81
Fl.
Cl.
Bsn.
Hn.
C Tpt.
Tbn.
Tba.
Timp.
Cym.
Choir
f
f
Vln. I
Vln. II
Vla.
Vc.
Db.

88

Fl.

Cl.

Bsn.

Hn.

C Tpt.

Tbn.

Tba.

Timp.

Cym.

mf

Choir

Vln. I

Vln. II

Vla.

Vc.

Db.

95
Fl.
Cl.
Bsn.
Hn.
C Tpt.
Tbn.
Tba.
Timp.
Cym.
Choir
mf
Vln. I
Vln. II
Vla.
Vc.
Db.

102
Fl.
Cl.
Bsn.
Hn.
C Tpt.
Tbn.
Tba.
Timp.
Cym.
Choir
Vln. I
Vln. II
Vla.
Vc.
Db.

111
Fl.
Cl.
Bsn.
Hn.
C Tpt.
Tbn.
Tba.
Timp.
3
3
3
Cym.
Choir
Vln. I
Vln. II
Vla.
Vc.
Db.

120
Fl.
Cl.
Bsn.
Hn.
C Tpt.
Tbn.
Tba.
Timp.
Cym.
Choir
Vln. I
Vln. II
Vla.
Vc.
Db.

126
Fl.
Cl.
Bsn.
Hn.
C Tpt.
Tbn.
Tba.
Timp.
Cym.
Choir
Vln. I
Vln. II
Vla.
Vc.
Db.

ACT III

Scene V – The Heart

Lorelle is dancing in the nursery with her new-born son laying in the crib and she is filled with joy for she has a beautiful strong boy who shall now be heir to the throne. Daethon enters and dances with her, still wearing the pendant as the Prince of Bourgogne. After dancing together, the Princess turns away to find a precious toy for the child. As she does so, Daethon lifts the child from his crib and holds him aloft holding his pendant in his hand. Lorelle turns and drops the toy in horror as she sees what he is doing. In a flash Gullveig and her Spirits appear and the Spirits dance around Lorelle and restrain her. She cries and pleads for mercy, that Gullveig not take her child, but Gullveig tells her that she still owes her a heart. She walks to Daethon and draws a dagger from within her raiment. Daethon hands her the child and with her back to all she walks towards the table. She places the child on the table and muttering magic she raises the dagger and drives it downwards to the scream of Lorelle. Gullveig turns and holds in her hand the child's bleeding heart. Laughing, she and the Spirits leave, as she holds the heart on high. Lorelle, beset with grief lies on the floor looking up in horror as the man she thought she loved walks away from her with the Spirits. Alone amongst all of them he is walking slowly backwards and meeting her gaze as he does so, and Lorelle reaches out in agonised grief as the scene ends with the dark red stain of blood.

Choreography, Costume and Set Notes

- The scene is now the nursery and needs to have an 18th century nursery feeling, so lace and pastel colours would look the part.

- Daethon enters in Bar 15 and initially the whole dance is about joyfully being with their child; it is only in Bar 35 when Lorelle turns away that darkness starts to loom and Daethon approaches the baby menacingly.

- He lifts the babe on high above his head baring his fangs as the music plays through Bars 36 to 38; Lorelle turns and drops the toy she is holding in horror before suddenly in Bar 39 the Spirits leap onto the stage and restrain her. The Spirits are now dressed in red, but their hearts and veins are still visible. In Bar 55 Gullveig appears and from Bar 63 she solemnly takes the baby to the table; she kills the child in Bar 71 to Lorelle's scream and then everything happens fast in Bars 72 and 73: Lorelle is thrown to the floor by the Spirits, they all scarper off stage as fast as they can, Gullveig walks off stage via upstage centre holding the heart triumphantly on high, leaving the audience watching Daethon walking away slowly backwards off stage as Lorelle looks at him in horror. He alone walks slowly and menacingly away; the others were all there just for the business of collecting the heart, but he was the one getting revenge.

- The lights go suddenly red for the murder and, at the end, Lorelle is left in a pool of dark red light before sudden darkness when the music ends.

♩ = 70
Flute
ppp
Oboe
Clarinet in B♭
Horn in F
Trumpet in B♭
Tuba
Timpani
Cymbals
Choir
Celesta
♩ = 70
Violin I
ppp
Violin II
ppp
Viola
ppp
Violoncello
Double Bass

3
Fl.
p
Ob.
Cl.
Hn.
Tpt.
Tba.
Timp.
Cym.
Choir
Cel.
p
Vln. I
Vln. II
Vla.
Vc.
Db.

6

Fl.

Ob.

Cl.

p

Hn.

p

Tpt.

Tba.

Timp.

Cym.

Choir

Cel.

Vln. I

Vln. II

Vla.

Vc.

Db.

9
Fl.
Ob.
Cl.
Hn.
mp
Tpt.
Tba.
Timp.
Cym.
Choir
Cel.
Vln. I
Vln. II
Vla.
Vc.
Db.

12
Fl.
Ob.
Cl.
Hn.
Tpt.
Tba.
Timp.
Cym.
Choir
Cel.
Vln. I
Vln. II
Vla.
Vc.
Db.

15
Fl.
Ob.
p
mp
Cl.
p
mp
Hn.
Tpt.
Tba.
Timp.
mp
Cym.
Choir
p
mp
Cel.
Vln. I
mp
Vln. II
pp
Vla.
pp
Vc.
pp
Db.

18

Fl.

Ob.

Cl.

Hn.

Tpt.

Tba.

Timp.

Cym.

Choir

Cel.

Vln. I

Vln. II

Vla.

Vc.

Db.

21
Fl.
Ob.
Cl.
Hn.
Tpt.
Tba.
Timp.
Cym.
Choir
mf
Cel.
p
Vln. I
Vln. II
Vla.
Vc.
Db.

24
Fl.
Ob.
Cl.
Hn.
Tpt.
Tba.
Timp.
Cym.
Choir
Cel.
Vln. I
Vln. II
Vla.
Vc.
Db.
tr
mp
mf
f
p
pp

27
Fl.
Ob.
Cl.
Hn.
Tpt.
Tba.
Timp.
Cym.
Choir
Cel.
Vln. I
Vln. II
Vla.
Vc.
Db.
f
mf
mp

30
Fl.
Ob.
Cl.
Hn.
Tpt.
Tba.
Timp.
Cym.
Choir
Cel.
Vln. I
Vln. II
Vla.
Vc.
Db.

33
Fl.
Ob.
Cl.
Hn.
Tpt.
Tba.
Timp.
Cym.
Choir
Cel.
Vln. I
Vln. II
Vla.
Vc.
Db.

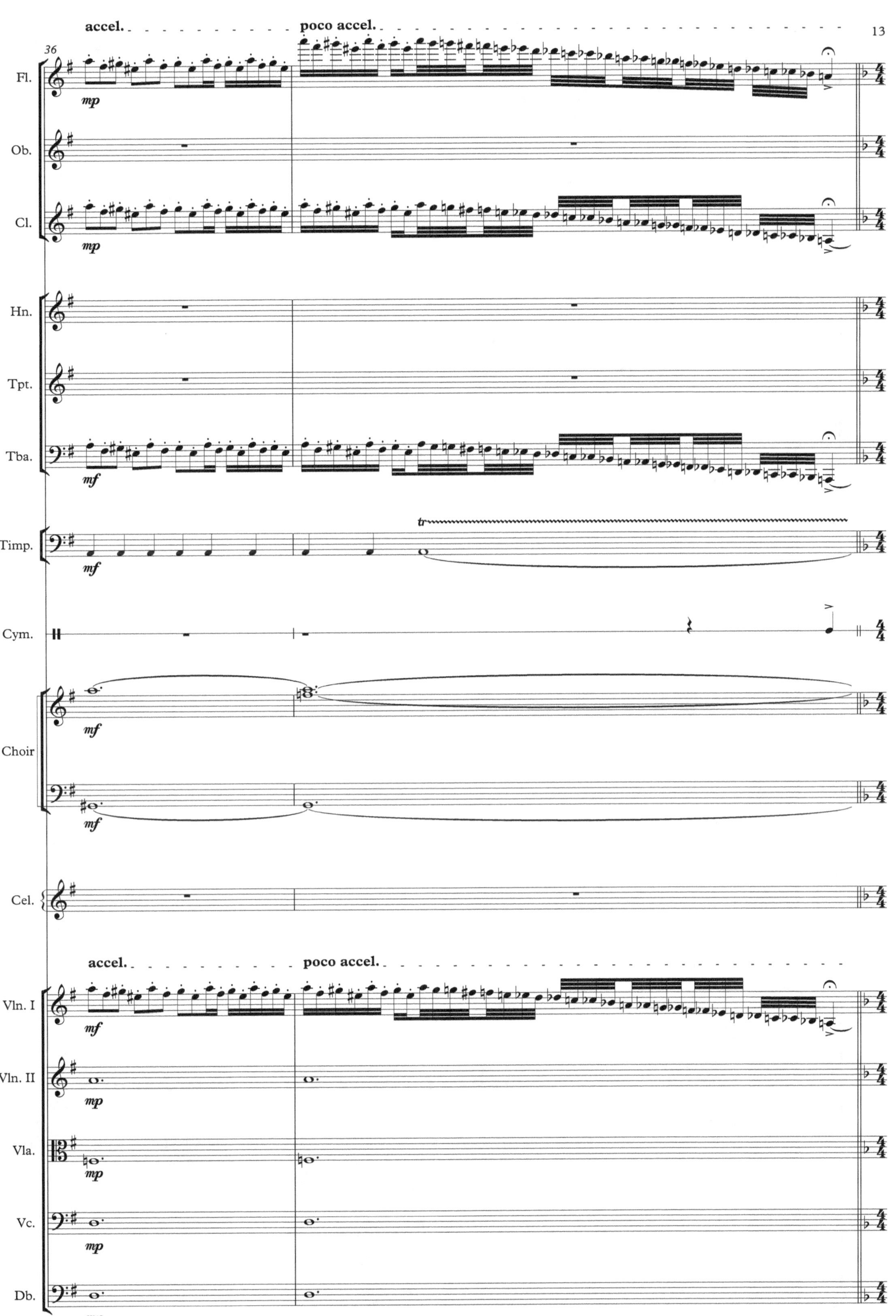
accel.
poco accel.
36
Fl.
Ob.
Cl.
Hn.
Tpt.
Tba.
Timp.
Cym.
Choir
Cel.
Vln. I
Vln. II
Vla.
Vc.
Db.
mp
mf
tr

♩ = 100
38
tr
Fl.
Ob.
Cl.
Hn.
Tpt.
Tba.
(tr)
Timp.
Cym.
Choir
Cel.
♩ = 100
tremolo
Vln. I
Vln. II
Vla.
Vc.
Db.
fff
f
mf

43

Fl.

Ob.

Cl.

Hn.

Tpt.

Tba.

Timp.

Cym.

Choir

Cel.

Vln. I

Vln. II

Vla.

Vc.

Db.

47
Fl.
Ob.
Cl.
Hn.
Tpt.
Tba.
Timp.
Cym.
Choir
Cel.
nat.
Vln. I
Vln. II
Vla.
Vc.
Db.

51
Fl.
Ob.
Cl.
Hn.
Tpt.
Tba.
Timp.
Cym.
Choir
Cel.
Vln. I
Vln. II
Vla.
Vc.
Db.

55
Fl.
Ob.
Cl.
Hn.
Tpt.
Tba.
Timp.
Cym.
Choir
Cel.
Vln. I
Vln. II
Vla.
Vc.
Db.

59
Fl.
Ob.
Cl.
Hn.
Tpt.
Tba.
Timp.
Cym.
Choir
Cel.
Vln. I
Vln. II
Vla.
Vc.
Db.

63
Fl.
mf
Ob.
mf
Cl.
Hn.
Tpt.
Tba.
Timp.
mf
Cym.
Choir
mf
mf
Cel.
Vln. I
mf
Vln. II
mf
Vla.
Vc.
mf
Db.
mf

67
Fl.
Ob.
Cl.
Hn.
Tpt.
Tba.
Timp.
Cym.
Choir
Cel.
Vln. I
Vln. II
Vla.
Vc.
Db.

69
Fl.
Ob.
Cl.
Hn.
Tpt.
Tba.
tr
Timp.
Cym.
Choir
Cel.
Vln. I
Vln. II
Vla.
Vc.
Db.
tremolo
fff
ff

ACT IV

ACT IV

Scene I – Arundel Returned

Gullveig is in her lair and rejoices with the Spirits at the new heart she has received. Suddenly during the festivities, Daethon arrives in their midst; he demands to receive what he has been promised, and Gullveig reluctantly agrees. She brings him to the centre of the chamber and begins her spell. To Daethon's joy, from a great mist, the beautiful Arundel rises again from the dead. The joy they both feel is unsurpassed and Gullveig and the Spirits recede to leave the two of them in the misty light. They dance together and renew all of the love that they had lost. Their joy is amazing to behold and as the scene ends, Arundel holds Daethon close and kisses him, with a passion that is beyond measure.

Choreography, Costume and Set Notes

- The scene starts again in the faerie kingdom, but great fires are now burning with copper powder in them to make them burn green.

- Daethon enters in Bar 83 and causes an abrupt stop to the dancing of Gullveig and the Spirits, demanding centre stage what he is owed.

- In Bars 91 to 98 Gullveig slowly approaches Daethon, initially menacingly but then softening – it is clear she intends to keep her promise; she takes his hand and the fires dull down and go out whilst the Spirits start to dance in a circle around a pale light growing in the centre of the stage. She raises her hands and begins to cast magic, and from the centre stage a great dry ice mist starts to billow forth. Then suddenly in Bar 109 Arundel becomes visible in the cloud of mist, either rising from beneath the stage or lowered down by wires from above, whichever works best visually. The two slowly come together reunited as Gullveig watches and the Spirits dance. They hold each other and kiss in the soft spotlight for a long time, all the way up to Bar 140, revelling in seeing each other again.

- From Bar 141 they move with Gullveig for all now to dance together for the finale. As the music steadily rises up to the climax at Bar 157 the Spirits one by one start to do fouetté turns; the spectacle of turns becoming more and more impressive and encompassing, up to the climax where both Daethon and Arundel are doing fouetté turns centre stage and the Spirits do jumps and acrobatics around them for the Grand Allegro moment of Bars 157 to 173, with it all ending triumphantly, but with sudden lights down to a spotlight on Arundel and Daethon

- In the last few bars of quiet slow music Arundel and Daethon come together in the spotlight; breathing hard they embrace and kiss and are reunited at last as the scene ends and the lights finally slowly go down.

♩ = 100
Flute
Oboe
Clarinet in B♭
Bassoon
Horn in F
Tuba
Timpani
Cymbals
Glockenspiel
♩ = 100
mp
Choir
mp
Violin I
Violin II
Viola
Violoncello
Double Bass

2
10
Fl.
Ob.
Cl.
Bsn.
Hn.
Tba.
Timp.
Cym.
Glock.
Choir
Vln. I
Vln. II
Vla.
Vc.
Db.

19
Fl.
Ob.
mf
Cl.
Bsn.
Hn.
Tba.
mf
Timp.
Cym.
Glock.
Choir
mf
mf
Vln. I
mf
Vln. II
mf
Vla.
mf
Vc.
mf
Db.
mf

28
Fl.
Ob.
Cl.
Bsn.
Hn.
Tba.
Timp.
Cym.
Glock.
Choir
Vln. I
Vln. II
Vla.
Vc.
Db.
mp

37

Fl.

Ob.

Cl.

Bsn.

Hn.

Tba.

Timp.

Cym.

Glock.

Choir

Vln. I

Vln. II

Vla.

Vc.

Db.

46
Fl.
Ob.
Cl.
Bsn.
Hn.
Tba.
Timp.
Cym.
Glock.
Choir
Vln. I
Vln. II
Vla.
Vc.
Db.

55
Fl.
Ob.
Cl.
Bsn.
Hn.
Tba.
Timp.
Cym.
Glock.
Choir
Vln. I
Vln. II
Vla.
Vc.
Db.

63
Fl.
Ob.
Cl.
Bsn.
Hn.
Tba.
Timp.
Cym.
Glock.
Choir
Vln. I
Vln. II
Vla.
Vc.
Db.
mp

72
Fl.
Ob.
Cl.
Bsn.
Hn.
Tba.
Timp.
Cym.
Glock.
Choir
Vln. I
Vln. II
Vla.
Vc.
Db.

81
Fl.
Ob.
Cl.
Bsn.
Hn.
Tba.
Timp.
Cym.
Glock.
Choir
Vln. I
Vln. II
Vla.
Vc.
Db.

90
Fl.
Ob.
Cl.
Bsn.
Hn.
pp
Tba.
Timp.
Cym.
Glock.
pp
Choir
Vln. I
Vln. II
Vla.
pp
Vc.
pp
Db.
pp

102
Fl.
Ob.
Cl.
Bsn.
Hn.
Tba.
tr
Timp.
Cym.
Glock.
Choir
Vln. I
mp
Vln. II
mp
Vla.
mp
Vc.
mp
Db.
mp

114
Fl.
Ob.
Cl.
Bsn.
Hn.
Tba.
Timp.
Cym.
Glock.
Choir
Vln. I
Vln. II
Vla.
Vc.
Db.

125
Fl.
Ob.
Cl.
Bsn.
Hn.
Tba.
Timp.
Cym.
Glock.
Choir
Vln. I
Vln. II
Vla.
Vc.
Db.

131
Fl.
Ob.
Cl.
Bsn.
Hn.
Tba.
Timp.
Cym.
Glock.
Choir
Vln. I
Vln. II
Vla.
Vc.
Db.

137
Fl.
Ob.
Cl.
Bsn.
Hn.
Tba.
Timp.
Cym.
Glock.
Choir
p
p
Vln. I
Vln. II
Vla.
p
Vc.
p
Db.
p

143
Fl.
Ob.
Cl.
Bsn.
Hn.
Tba.
Timp.
Cym.
Glock.
Choir
Vln. I
Vln. II
Vla.
Vc.
Db.

149
Fl.
Ob.
Cl.
Bsn.
Hn.
Tba.
Timp.
Cym.
Glock.
mf
Choir
mf
Vln. I
Vln. II
mf
Vla.
mf
Vc.
mf
Db.

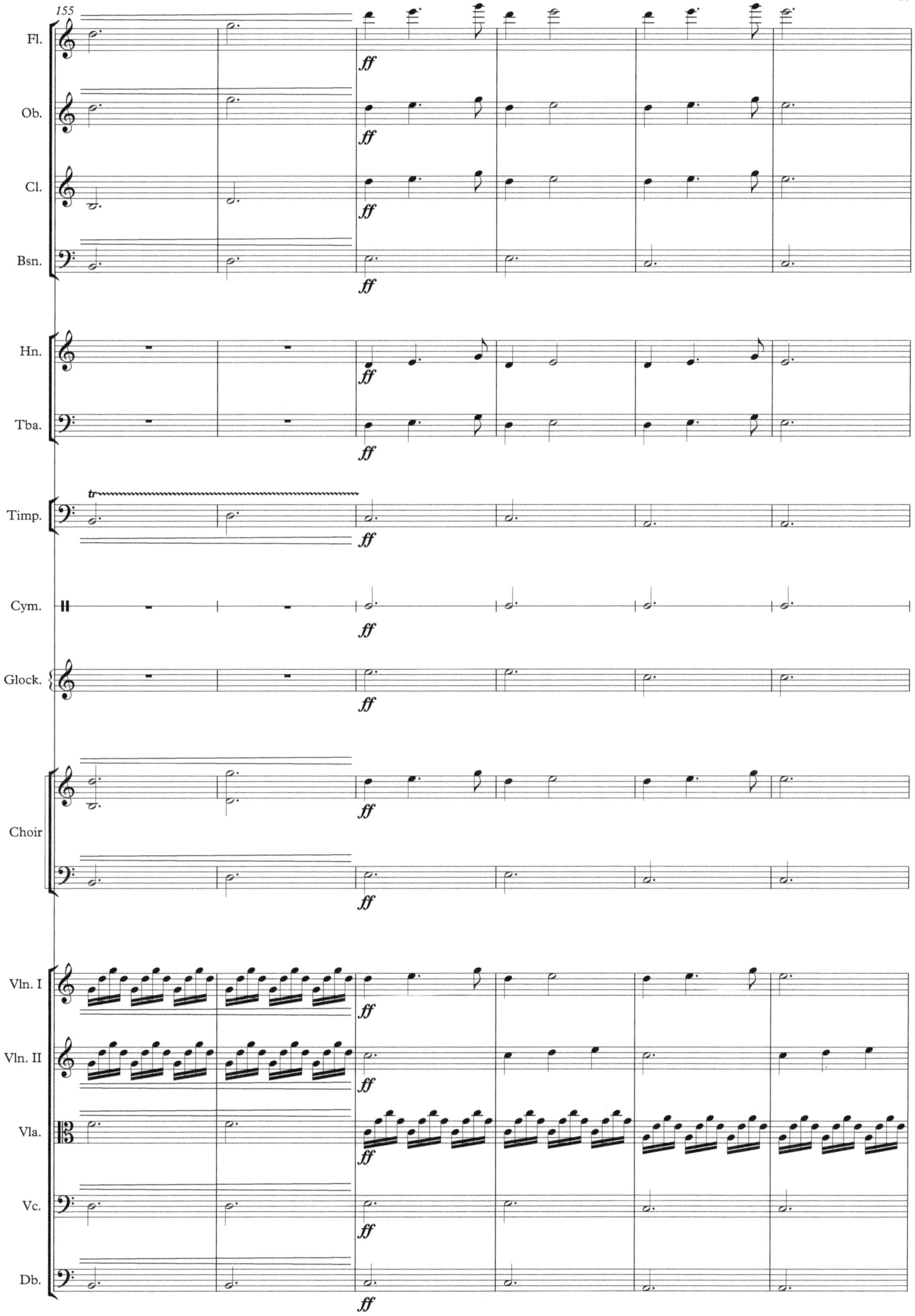
155
Fl.
Ob.
Cl.
Bsn.
Hn.
Tba.
Timp.
tr
Cym.
Glock.
Choir
Vln. I
Vln. II
Vla.
Vc.
Db.
ff

161
Fl.
Ob.
Cl.
Bsn.
Hn.
Tba.
Timp.
Cym.
Glock.
Choir
Vln. I
Vln. II
Vla.
Vc.
Db.

167
Fl.
Ob.
Cl.
Bsn.
Hn.
Tba.
Timp.
tr
Cym.
Glock.
Choir
Vln. I
Vln. II
Vla.
Vc.
Db.

173
molto rall.
Fl.
Ob.
Cl.
Bsn.
Hn.
Tba.
(tr)
Timp.
Cym.
Glock.
pp
molto rall.
pp
Choir
Vln. I
ppp
Vln. II
pp
Vla.
Vc.
ppp
Db.
pp

ACT IV

Scene II – In the Court of the King

King Haelan is holding a dull and subdued court; his daughter has lost her child to an assailant she will not name, whilst his heir, the Prince of Bourgogne, is missing. The Nobles try to entertain him, some even dressed as jesters and prancing most gaily, but he cannot be raised from his sadness. Thereupon a trumpet sounds and Arundel and Daethon enter the court. None can believe their eyes at the miracle and the king himself falls to his knees to see his son restored from death. He asks how this can be, but Arundel can only say that the magical powers that have restored him are beyond his comprehension, but that Daethon has done this thing. King Haelan weeps with joy, embraces Daethon as a son and the Nobles begin to celebrate. The raucous joy rises to an amazing climax as King Haelan watches happily from his throne as his son dances with his saviour Daethon, with all the Nobles and their Ladies joining in. As the festivities die down, Daethon and Arundel dance a pas de deux. However, in the last moment the figure of Lorelle appears watching them, and her eyes are filled with fury, though they do not see her. Behind her the dark figure of a man, who will later be revealed to be Macon the Blacksmith, appears menacingly and they stand there together watching, before leaving with dark fury as the duet ends.

Choreography, Costume and Set Notes

- The trumpet sounds in Bars 81 to 82 to herald the arrival of Daethon and Arundel, dressed in their blue and white as before; before this the Nobles and Ladies have tried various styles of dance to amuse the king in something of a divertissement style.

- The pas de deux is from Bar 153 to the end of the music and is danced with a spotlight on Daethon and Arundel; from Bar 196 however, in one corner of upstage, Lorelle, and then Macon behind her, appear looking on in a deep red spotlight before leaving stage just before the scene ends. The scene thus ends with just the original white spotlight on Daethon and Arundel but the lingering memory of the previous light.

♩ = 60
♩ = 80
molto accel.
Piccolo
Flute
Oboe
Clarinet in B♭
Bass Clarinet in B♭
Contrabassoon
Trumpet in C
Trumpet in B♭
Trombone
Timpani
Cymbals
Violin I
Violin II
Viola
Violoncello
Double Bass
pp
mp
ppp

♩ = 125
18
Picc.
Fl.
Ob.
Cl.
B. Cl.
Cbsn.
C Tpt.
Tpt.
Tbn.
Timp.
Cym.
Vln. I
Vln. II
Vla.
Vc.
Db.
pp
mp

30

Picc.

Fl.

Ob.

Cl.

B. Cl.

Cbsn.

C Tpt.

Tpt.

Tbn.

Timp.

Cym.

Vln. I

Vln. II

Vla.

Vc.

Db.

mf *f*

42
Picc.
Fl.
Ob.
Cl.
B. Cl.
Cbsn.
C Tpt.
Tpt.
Tbn.
Timp.
Cym.
Vln. I
Vln. II
Vla.
Vc.
Db.
f
mp
mp
mp
mp
mp

54

Picc.

Fl.

Ob.

Cl.

B. Cl.

Cbsn.

C Tpt.

Tpt.

Tbn.

Timp.

Cym.

Vln. I

Vln. II

Vla.

Vc.

Db.

64
Picc.
Fl.
Ob.
Cl.
B. Cl.
Cbsn.
C Tpt.
Tpt.
Tbn.
Timp.
Cym.
Vln. I
mf
Vln. II
mf
Vla.
Vc.
Db.

75
♩ = 60
molto accel.
Picc.
Fl.
Ob.
Cl.
B. Cl.
Cbsn.
C Tpt.
Tpt.
Tbn.
Timp.
Cym.
Vln. I
Vln. II
Vla.
Vc.
Db.
mp
ff

87
molto rall.
Picc.
Fl.
Ob.
mp
Cl.
mp
B. Cl.
mp
Cbsn.
C Tpt.
mp
Tpt.
mp
Tbn.
Timp.
molto rall.
Cym.
Vln. I
mp
Vln. II
mp
Vla.
mp
Vc.
Db.

♩ = 125

99

Picc.
Fl.
Ob.
Cl.
B. Cl.
Cbsn.
C Tpt.
Tpt.
Tbn.
Timp.

♩ = 125

Cym.
Vln. I
Vln. II
Vla.
Vc.
Db.

110
Picc.
Fl.
Ob.
Cl.
B. Cl.
Cbsn.
C Tpt.
Tpt.
Tbn.
Timp.
Cym.
Vln. I
Vln. II
Vla.
Vc.
Db.
f
mf
mp

122
Picc.
Fl.
Ob.
Cl.
B. Cl.
Cbsn.
C Tpt.
Tpt.
Tbn.
Timp.
Cym.
Vln. I
Vln. II
Vla.
Vc.
Db.
f
mp
mp

132
Picc.
Fl.
Ob.
Cl.
B. Cl.
Cbsn.
C Tpt.
Tpt.
Tbn.
Timp.
Cym.
Vln. I
Vln. II
Vla.
Vc.
Db.
ff
f

♩ = 60
142
Picc.
Fl.
Ob.
Cl.
ppp
B. Cl.
ppp
Cbsn.
ppp
C Tpt.
Tpt.
Tbn.
Timp.
tr
♩ = 60
Cym.
Vln. I
Vln. II
Vla.
Vc.
Db.

154
Picc.
Fl.
p
Ob.
Cl.
pp
B. Cl.
pp
Cbsn.
pp
C Tpt.
Tpt.
Tbn.
Timp.
Cym.
Vln. I
Vln. II
Vla.
ppp
pp
Vc.
Db.

159
Picc.
Fl.
Ob.
Cl.
B. Cl.
Cbsn.
C Tpt.
Tpt.
Tbn.
Timp.
Cym.
Vln. I
Vln. II
ppp
Vla.
Vc.
Db.

165
Picc.
Fl.
Ob.
Cl.
B. Cl.
Cbsn.
C Tpt.
Tpt.
Tbn.
Timp.
Cym.
Vln. I
Vln. II
Vla.
Vc.
Db.

171
Picc.
Fl.
Ob.
Cl.
B. Cl.
Cbsn.
C Tpt.
Tpt.
Tbn.
Timp.
Cym.
Vln. I
Vln. II
Vla.
Vc.
Db.
p
p
ppp
ppp

177
Picc.
Fl.
Ob.
Cl.
B. Cl.
Cbsn.
C Tpt.
Tpt.
Tbn.
Timp.
Cym.
Vln. I
Vln. II
Vla.
Vc.
Db.
mf

182
Picc.
Fl.
Ob.
Cl.
B. Cl.
Cbsn.
C Tpt.
Tpt.
Tbn.
Timp.
Cym.
Vln. I
Vln. II
Vla.
Vc.
Db.

187
Picc.
Fl.
Ob.
Cl.
B. Cl.
Cbsn.
C Tpt.
Tpt.
Tbn.
tr
Timp.
Cym.
Vln. I
Vln. II
Vla.
Vc.
Db.

192
Picc.
Fl.
Ob.
Cl.
B. Cl.
Cbsn.
C Tpt.
Tpt.
Tbn.
Timp.
Cym.
Vln. I
Vln. II
Vla.
Vc.
Db.

197
Picc.
Fl.
Ob.
Cl.
B. Cl.
Cbsn.
C Tpt.
Tpt.
Tbn.
Timp.
Cym.
Vln. I
Vln. II
Vla.
Vc.
Db.

200
rall.
Picc.
Fl.
Ob.
Cl.
B. Cl.
Cbsn.
C Tpt.
Tpt.
Tbn.
Timp.
rall.
Cym.
Vln. I
Vln. II
Vla.
Vc.
Db.

ACT IV

Scene III – Murder in the Town Square

Arundel and Daethon are filled with joy and the next day they walk in the Town Square, watching the people going by. Arundel gets down on one knee and professes his love to Daethon, by the great fountain in the centre of the square. Meanwhile by a market stall, Lorelle stands, hooded, by the figure of Macon the Blacksmith. She passes him some coins and leaves the scene. Then as Arundel and Daethon continue to walk around the square, Macon begins to follow Daethon. Of a sudden, Macon sneaks up right behind Daethon and drives a stake into his heart. Daethon falls to the ground stabbed and Arundel immediately draws his sword, fights Macon and runs him through, but it is too late. Daethon lies dying on the steps of the fountain and the nobles in the square gather around as Arundel holds Daethon close as he dies and weeps, and as Daethon finally passes away, the music changes to a funeral march and Arundel lifts Daethon's body in his arms, carrying him off stage with the help of the townspeople and the nobles who have come to the terrible scene.

Choreography, Costume and Set Notes

- The murder is committed in Bar 70 and must be a wooden stake through the heart since Daethon of course is a Vampire.
- The fight scene between Arundel and Macon is then with swords up to Bar 81 where Arundel finally kills him.
- Arundel then drops his sword and runs to lift Daethon's upper body in his arms; they have a moment of love together as the mournful music plays just before Daethon dies and the townsfolk slowly gather round in support and sadness, with Nobles and Ladies joining them; the lighting now focuses on the death: having been a warm sunny glow before it is now sharp white light. The fight scene can be lit extravagantly as well.
- The funeral march offstage is from Bar 123 to the end of the scene.

♩ = 80
Flute
Oboe
Trumpet in B♭
Trombone
Tuba
Timpani
Cymbals
Harp
gliss.
f
mf
Choir
Celesta
p
♩ = 80
tremolo
nat.
Violin I
ppp
pp
Violin II
Viola
pp
Violoncello
Double Bass

8
Fl.
Ob.
Tpt.
Tbn.
Tba.
Timp.
Cym.
Hp.
Choir
Cel.
Vln. I
Vln. II
ppp
Vla.
Vc.
ppp
p
Db.
ppp
p

14
Fl.
Ob.
Tpt.
Tbn.
Tba.
Timp.
Cym.
Hp.
Choir
Cel.
Vln. I
Vln. II
Vla.
p
Vc.
Db.

20
Fl.
mf
3
3
Ob.
Tpt.
Tbn.
Tba.
Timp.
Cym.
Hp.
Choir
Cel.
p
Vln. I
mf
p
Vln. II
p
Vla.
Vc.
Db.

25
Fl.
Ob.
Tpt.
Tbn.
Tba.
Timp.
Cym.
Hp.
Choir
Cel.
Vln. I
Vln. II
Vla.
Vc.
Db.

30
Fl.
Ob.
Tpt.
Tbn.
Tba.
Timp.
Cym.
Hp.
Choir
Cel.
Vln. I
Vln. II
Vla.
Vc.
Db.

35
Fl.
Ob.
mf
3
Tpt.
Tbn.
Tba.
Timp.
Cym.
Hp.
mp
Choir
mp
Cel.
Vln. I
mp
3
Vln. II
mp
Vla.
mp
Vc.
mp
Db.
mp

40
Fl.
Ob.
Tpt.
Tbn.
Tba.
Timp.
Cym.
Hp.
Choir
Cel.
Vln. I
Vln. II
Vla.
Vc.
Db.

45
Fl.
Ob.
Tpt.
Tbn.
Tba.
Timp.
Cym.
Hp.
Choir
Cel.
Vln. I
Vln. II
Vla.
Vc.
Db.

50
Fl.
Ob.
Tpt.
Tbn.
Tba.
Timp.
Cym.
Hp.
Choir
Cel.
Vln. I
Vln. II
Vla.
Vc.
Db.
p
mf
pp
3

55

Fl.

Ob.

Tpt.

Tbn.

Tba.

Timp.

Cym.

Hp.

Choir

Cel.

Vln. I

Vln. II

Vla.

Vc.

Db.

59
Fl.
Ob.
Tpt.
Tbn.
Tba.
Timp.
Cym.
Hp.
Choir
Cel.
Vln. I
Vln. II
Vla.
Vc.
Db.

63
Fl.
Ob.
Tpt.
Tbn.
Tba.
Timp.
Cym.
Hp.
Choir
Cel.
Vln. I
Vln. II
Vla.
Vc.
Db.

67
♩ = 100
Fl.
Ob.
Tpt.
Tbn.
Tba.
Timp.
Cym.
Hp.
Choir
Cel.
Vln. I
Vln. II
Vla.
Vc.
Db.

71
(tr)
Fl.
Ob.
Tpt.
Tbn.
Tba.
Timp.
Cym.
Hp.
Choir
Cel.
Vln. I
Vln. II
Vla.
Vc.
Db.
fff
f
gliss.

74
Fl.
Ob.
Tpt.
Tbn.
Tba.
Timp.
Cym.
Hp.
Choir
Cel.
Vln. I
Vln. II
Vla.
Vc.
Db.

76
Fl.
Ob.
Tpt.
Tbn.
Tba.
Timp.
Cym.
Hp.
Choir
Cel.
Vln. I
Vln. II
Vla.
Vc.
Db.

78
Fl.
Ob.
Tpt.
Tbn.
Tba.
Timp.
tr
Cym.
Hp.
Choir
Cel.
Vln. I
Vln. II
Vla.
Vc.
Db.

80
♩ = 60
Fl.
Ob.
nat.
ppp
Tpt.
Tbn.
Tba.
tr
(tr)
Timp.
Cym.
Hp.
p
Choir
Cel.
♩ = 60
nat.
tremolo
Vln. I
ppp
tremolo
Vln. II
Vla.
ppp
Vc.
Db.
p

85
Fl.
Ob.
Tpt.
Tbn.
Tba.
Timp.
Cym.
Hp.
Choir
Cel.
Vln. I
Vln. II
Vla.
Vc.
ppp
Db.
ppp

90
Fl.
Ob.
Tpt.
Tbn.
Tba.
Timp.
Cym.
Hp.
Choir
Cel.
Vln. I
Vln. II
Vla.
Vc.
Db.

95
Fl.
Ob.
Tpt.
Tbn.
Tba.
Timp.
Cym.
Hp.
Choir
Cel.
Vln. I
Vln. II
Vla.
Vc.
Db.
mp
mp
nat.
ppp
pp
pp
pp
pp
pp

100
Fl.
Ob.
Tpt.
Tbn.
Tba.
Timp.
Cym.
Hp.
Choir
Cel.
Vln. I
Vln. II
Vla.
Vc.
Db.

106
Fl.
Ob.
mp
Tpt.
Tbn.
Tba.
Timp.
Cym.
Hp.
Choir
p
Cel.
Vln. I
Vln. II
Vla.
Vc.
Db.

112
Fl.
Ob.
Tpt.
Tbn.
Tba.
Timp.
Cym.
Hp.
Choir
Cel.
Vln. I
Vln. II
Vla.
Vc.
Db.

118
Fl.
Ob.
Tpt.
Tbn.
Tba.
Timp.
Cym.
Hp.
Choir
Cel.
Vln. I
Vln. II
Vla.
Vc.
Db.
3
mp

125
Fl.
Ob.
Tpt.
Tbn.
Tba.
Timp.
Cym.
Hp.
Choir
Cel.
Vln. I
Vln. II
Vla.
Vc.
Db.

132
Fl.
Ob.
Tpt.
Tbn.
Tba.
Timp.
Cym.
Hp.
Choir
Cel.
Vln. I
Vln. II
Vla.
Vc.
Db.

ACT IV

Scene IV – Walking in the Garden

Time has passed, and the music plays for a time to the curtain to emphasise this before the scene opens to Arundel walking in the Garden by the tomb that has been erected to Daethon. He kneels and weeps after laying flowers and dancing in sadness around the Garden, beset still with grief. As he kneels weeping, the Lady Nerida enters with her ladies all in ballerina tutus, chatting and laughing following their dance practice together. She and they stop when they see him, and as the Lady Nerida approaches and comforts Arundel, the ladies dance in a mournful and apologetic corps; in the end, the two of them dance together in friendship as she brings some light back to his life. She always stood by him and through the dance he shows her that he would be willing to marry her again and sire an heir to continue King Haelan's line. She brings him to Daethon's tomb and places flowers of her own brought by one of her ladies before they walk out of the garden solemnly, aware of how dark the fate is that has brought them now to this point.

Choreography, Costume and Set Notes

- The music for this scene initially plays to darkness, then to a lit closed curtain before the curtain finally opens; this is intended to convey the passage of time before the curtain opens in Bar 21. Nerida and the ladies do not enter until Bar 53.

- The choreographer has great freedom here to create any form of mournful adagio but the key with Arundel's character is his continuous return to grief, so throughout the dance Nerida must struggle with him and he must stumble at times back to the grave and weep.

♩ = 100
Piccolo
Flute
Oboe
Clarinet in B♭
Bassoon
Timpani
Cymbals
Harp
Celesta
♩ = 100
Violin I
Violin II
pp
Viola
mp
Violoncello
mp
Double Bass
mp

9
Picc.
Fl.
Ob.
Cl.
Bsn.
Timp.
Cym.
Hp.
Cel.
Vln. I
Vln. II
mp
Vla.
Vc.
Db.

18
Picc.
Fl.
Ob.
Cl.
Bsn.
Timp.
Cym.
Hp.
Cel.
Vln. I
Vln. II
Vla.
Vc.
Db.

27
Picc.
Fl.
Ob.
Cl.
Bsn.
Timp.
Cym.
Hp.
Cel.
Vln. I
Vln. II
Vla.
Vc.
Db.

36
Picc.
Fl.
Ob.
Cl.
Bsn.
Timp.
Cym.
Hp.
Cel.
Vln. I
Vln. II
Vla.
Vc.
Db.

45
Picc.
Fl.
Ob.
Cl.
Bsn.
Timp.
Cym.
Hp.
Cel.
Vln. I
Vln. II
Vla.
Vc.
Db.

54
Picc.
Fl.
Ob.
Cl.
Bsn.
Timp.
Cym.
Hp.
Cel.
Vln. I
Vln. II
Vla.
Vc.
Db.

63
Picc.
Fl.
Ob.
Cl.
Bsn.
Timp.
Cym.
Hp.
Cel.
Vln. I
Vln. II
Vla.
Vc.
Db.

71

Picc.
Fl.
Ob.
Cl.
Bsn.
Timp.
Cym.
Hp.
Cel.
Vln. I
Vln. II
Vla.
Vc.
Db.

79

Picc.

Fl.

Ob.

Cl.

Bsn.

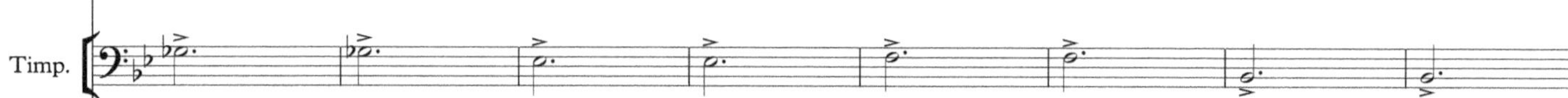

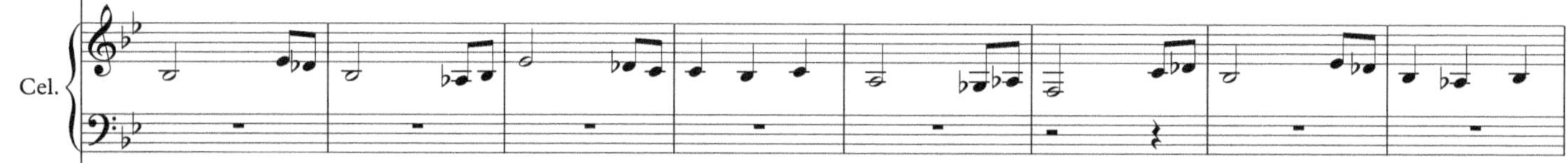

87

Picc.

Fl.

Ob.

Cl.

Bsn.

Timp.

Cym.

Hp.

Cel.

Vln. I

Vln. II

Vla.

Vc.

Db.

96
Picc.
Fl.
Ob.
Cl.
Bsn.
Timp.
Cym.
Hp.
Cel.
Vln. I
Vln. II
Vla.
Vc.
Db.

105
Picc.
Fl.
Ob.
Cl.
Bsn.
Timp.
Cym.
Hp.
Cel.
Vln. I
Vln. II
Vla.
Vc.
Db.

114
Picc.
Fl.
Ob.
Cl.
Bsn.
tr
Timp.
Cym.
Hp.
Cel.
Vln. I
Vln. II
Vla.
Vc.
Db.

123
rall.
Picc.
Fl.
Ob.
Cl.
Bsn.
Timp.
Cym.
Hp.
Cel.
rall.
Vln. I
Vln. II
Vla.
Vc.
Db.

128
Picc.
Fl.
Ob.
Cl.
Bsn.
Timp.
tr
Cym.
Hp.
Cel.
Vln. I
Vln. II
Vla.
Vc.
Db.

ACT IV

Scene V – A Last Dance

It is Arundel and the Lady Nerida's wedding day – they are married with great celebration and they dance together an amazing dance with all the court. At the end of the night when all the festivities have died down, Arundel is alone in the court, with all others having left. He dreams, and in his mind's eye he sees Daethon. He dances with him and together in his imagination they dance with all the love that he feels for Daethon. At the end, Daethon slowly walks away but stops for a moment and bows low in farewell. Arundel watches as Daethon walks away into the bright light of the moon, filling his eyes with light and joy at this, the climax of their story, as at last Daethon fades and Arundel sinks to his knees with one arm outstretched to finally say farewell to the man he loves more than any other on this earth.

Choreography, Costume and Set Notes

- This is the climax of the entire ballet so the dance of the corps must be a spectacle to behold; the scene starts outside the ballroom, before the great doors, where the Lady Nerida comforts Arundel with a hand to his cheek before they go in; the doors are guarded by two guards, one on either side and as they open the doors in Bar 41 the walls separate or lift away to show the entire scene behind, filled with lords and ladies dancing.

- The dance reaches an amazing climax in Bars 105 through to 137 and then all solemnly leave as a spotlight centres on Arundel after he has given Nerida a small kiss before she leaves. Arundel is left alone now in the great ballroom, which should be decorated with side tables and chandeliers in the fashion you might expect. Lit by the spotlight he dances alone in sadness, before in Bar 203 he collapses to the ground weeping; then suddenly Daethon appears upstage centre in a second light in Bar 219 before they dance their final pas de deux together, expressing their love again at last. In Bar 267 Daethon turns to leave and walks away before making his bow in the rallentando, as Arundel slowly comes down to the floor. The scene ends with Arundel in a soft spotlight alone on stage on the floor, with arm outstretched, before the lights go down and the ballet finishes.

♩ = 175
Piccolo
Flute
Oboe
Clarinet in B♭
Horn in F
Trumpet in B♭
Tuba
Timpani
Cymbals
Harp
♩ = 175
Violin I
Violin II
Viola
Violoncello
Double Bass

10
Picc.
Fl.
Ob.
Cl.
Hn.
Tpt.
Tba.
Timp.
Cym.
Hp.
Vln. I
Vln. II
Vla.
Vc.
Db.

20
Picc.
Fl.
Ob.
Cl.
Hn.
Tpt.
Tba.
Timp.
Cym.
Hp.
Vln. I
Vln. II
Vla.
Vc.
Db.

30

Picc.

Fl.

Ob.

Cl.

Hn.

Tpt.

Tba.

Timp.

tr

Cym.

Hp.

Vln. I

Vln. II

Vla.

Vc.

Db.

40
Picc.
Fl.
Ob.
Cl.
Hn.
Tpt.
Tba.
Timp.
Cym.
Hp.
Vln. I
Vln. II
Vla.
Vc.
Db.
mf
(tr)

50
Picc.
Fl.
Ob.
Cl.
Hn.
Tpt.
Tba.
Timp.
Cym.
Hp.
Vln. I
Vln. II
Vla.
Vc.
Db.

60

Picc.

Fl.

Ob.

Cl.

Hn.

Tpt.

Tba.

Timp.

Cym.

Hp.

Vln. I

Vln. II

Vla.

Vc.

Db.

70

Picc. *f*

Fl. *f*

Ob. *f*

Cl. *f*

Hn. *f*

Tpt. *f*

Tba. *f*

Timp. *f*

Cym. *f*

Hp.

Vln. I *f*

Vln. II *f*

Vla. *f*

Vc. *f*

Db. *f*

80
Picc.
Fl.
Ob.
Cl.
Hn.
Tpt.
Tba.
Timp.
Cym.
Hp.
Vln. I
Vln. II
Vla.
Vc.
Db.
mf
ppp
mp
mp
mp
mp

90
Picc.
Fl.
Ob.
Cl.
Hn.
Tpt.
Tba.
Timp.
Cym.
Hp.
Vln. I
Vln. II
Vla.
Vc.
Db.

100

Picc.

Fl.

Ob.

Cl.

Hn.

Tpt.

Tba.

Timp.

Cym.

Hp.

Vln. I

Vln. II

Vla.

Vc.

Db.

mp *ff*

tr

110

Picc.

Fl.

Ob.

Cl.

Hn.

Tpt.

Tba.

Timp.

Cym.

Hp.

Vln. I

Vln. II

Vla.

Vc.

Db.

120
molto rall.
Picc.
Fl.
Ob.
Cl.
Hn.
Tpt.
Tba.
Timp.
Cym.
Hp.
molto rall.
Vln. I
Vln. II
Vla.
Vc.
Db.

130
♩ = 115
Picc.
Fl.
Ob.
Cl.
Hn.
Tpt.
Tba.
Timp.
tr
Cym.
Hp.
Vln. I
Vln. II
Vla.
Vc.
Db.
p

140
Picc.
Fl.
Ob.
Cl.
Hn.
Tpt.
Tba.
Timp.
Cym.
Hp.
Vln. I
Vln. II
Vla.
Vc.
Db.

147

Picc.

Fl.

Ob.

Cl.

Hn.

Tpt.

Tba.

Timp.

Cym.

Hp.

Vln. I

Vln. II

Vla.

Vc.

Db.

154
Picc.
Fl.
Ob.
mp
Cl.
Hn.
Tpt.
Tba.
Timp.
Cym.
Hp.
Vln. I
Vln. II
Vla.
Vc.
Db.

161
Picc.
Fl.
Ob.
Cl.
Hn.
Tpt.
Tba.
Timp.
Cym.
Hp.
Vln. I
Vln. II
Vla.
Vc.
Db.

168
Picc.
Fl.
mp
Ob.
Cl.
Hn.
Tpt.
Tba.
Timp.
Cym.
Hp.
Vln. I
Vln. II
Vla.
Vc.
Db.

175
Picc.
Fl.
Ob.
Cl.
Hn.
Tpt.
Tba.
Timp.
Cym.
Hp.
Vln. I
Vln. II
Vla.
Vc.
Db.

182
Picc.
Fl.
Ob.
Cl.
Hn.
Tpt.
Tba.
Timp.
Cym.
Hp.
Vln. I
Vln. II
Vla.
Vc.
Db.
mp
mp
mp
mp

189

Picc.

Fl.

Ob.

Cl.

Hn.

Tpt.

Tba.

Timp.

Cym.

Hp.

Vln. I

Vln. II

Vla.

Vc.

Db.

196
Picc.
Fl.
Ob.
Cl.
Hn.
Tpt.
Tba.
Timp.
Cym.
Hp.
Vln. I
Vln. II
Vla.
Vc.
Db.

203
Picc.
Fl.
Ob.
Cl.
Hn.
Tpt.
Tba.
Timp.
Cym.
Hp.
p
Vln. I
Vln. II
Vla.
Vc.
Db.

210
Picc.
Fl.
Ob.
Cl.
Hn.
Tpt.
Tba.
Timp.
Cym.
Hp.
Vln. I
Vln. II
Vla.
Vc.
Db.

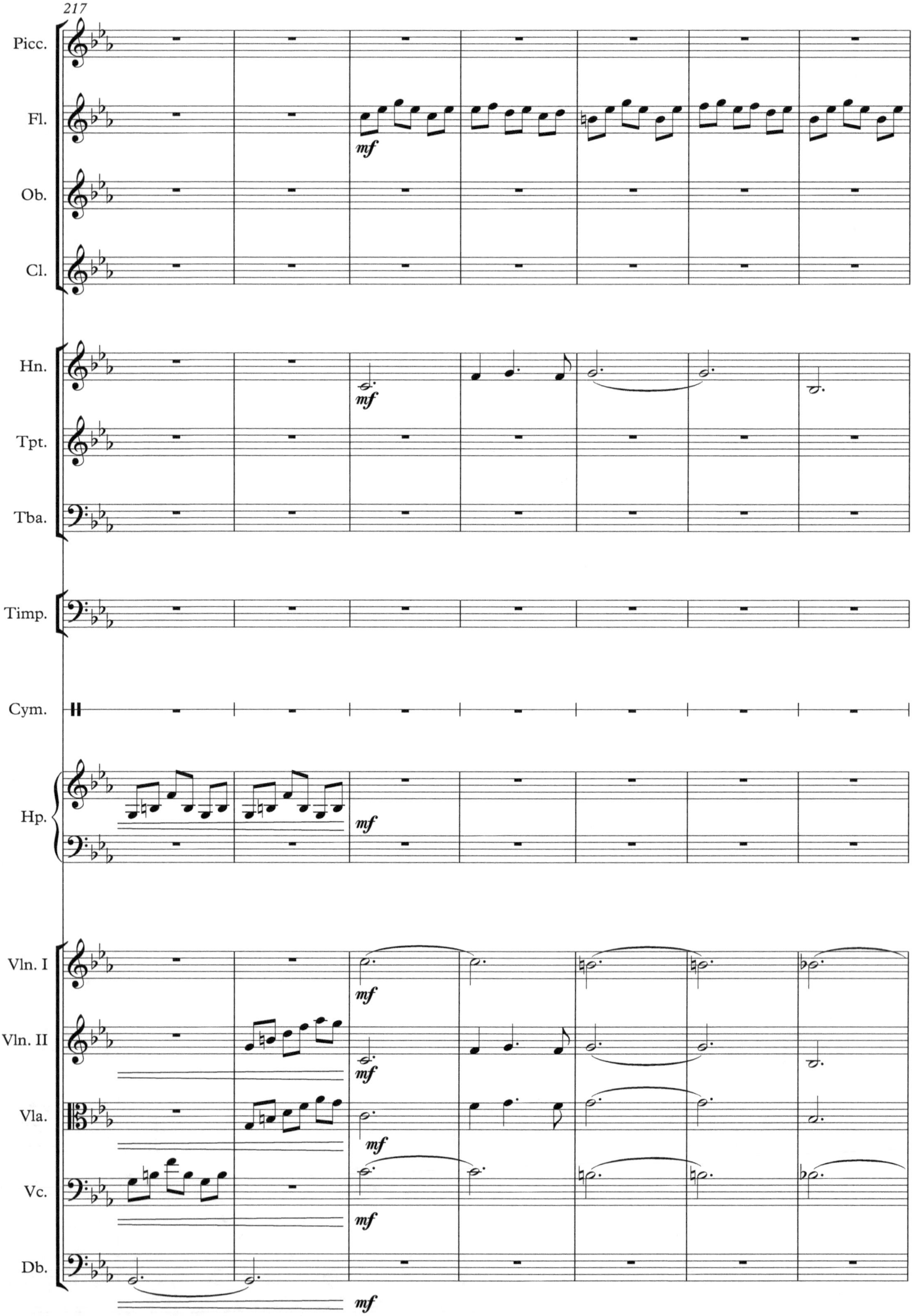
217
Picc.
Fl.
mf
Ob.
Cl.
Hn.
mf
Tpt.
Tba.
Timp.
Cym.
Hp.
mf
Vln. I
mf
Vln. II
mf
Vla.
mf
Vc.
mf
Db.
mf

224
Picc.
Fl.
Ob.
Cl.
Hn.
Tpt.
Tba.
Timp.
Cym.
Hp.
Vln. I
Vln. II
Vla.
Vc.
Db.

231
Picc.
Fl.
Ob.
Cl.
Hn.
Tpt.
Tba.
Timp.
Cym.
Hp.
Vln. I
Vln. II
Vla.
Vc.
Db.
f
mf
tr

238
Picc.
Fl.
Ob.
Cl.
Hn.
Tpt.
Tba.
Timp.
Cym.
Hp.
Vln. I
Vln. II
Vla.
Vc.
Db.

245
Picc.
Fl.
Ob.
Cl.
Hn.
Tpt.
Tba.
Timp.
Cym.
Hp.
Vln. I
Vln. II
Vla.
Vc.
Db.
mp

252
Picc.
Fl.
Ob.
Cl.
Hn.
Tpt.
Tba.
Timp.
Cym.
Hp.
Vln. I
Vln. II
Vla.
Vc.
Db.

259
Picc.
Fl.
Ob.
Cl.
Hn.
Tpt.
Tba.
Timp.
Cym.
Hp.
Vln. I
Vln. II
Vla.
Vc.
Db.

266
Picc.
Fl.
Ob.
Cl.
Hn.
Tpt.
Tba.
Timp.
Cym.
Hp.
Vln. I
Vln. II
Vla.
Vc.
Db.
mf
f

273
molto rall.
Picc.
Fl.
Ob.
Cl.
Hn.
Tpt.
Tba.
Timp.
Cym.
Hp.
molto rall.
Vln. I
Vln. II
Vla.
Vc.
Db.

278
Picc.
Fl.
Ob.
Cl.
Hn.
Tpt.
Tba.
Timp.
Cym.
Hp.
Vln. I
Vln. II
Vla.
Vc.
Db.
p
pp
tr

FIN

www.ingramcontent.com/pod-product-compliance
Lightning Source LLC
Chambersburg PA
CBHW080909230426
43665CB00019B/2552